T0108049

I WONDERED ABOUT THAT TOO

Copyright © 2018 Larry Scheckel

All rights reserved. No part of this book may be used or reproduced, stored in a retrieval system, or transmitted by any means - electronic, mechanical, photocopying, recording or in any manner whatsoever without written permission from the publisher except in the case of brief quotations embodied in critical articles and reviews.

For further information, contact:
Tumblehome, Inc.
201 Newbury St, Suite 201
Boston, MA 02116
http://www.Thinc-science.org

Library of Congress Control Number: 2018953807
ISBN 978-1-943431-38-0

Scheckel, Larry
I Wondered About That Too / Larry Scheckel - 1st ed

Front cover science & technology icons: designed by Freepik from Flaticon
Front and back cover images: Courtesy NASA/JPL-Caltech (modified)

Printed in Taiwan

10 9 8 7 6 5 4 3 2 1

I WONDERED
ABOUT THAT TOO

*111 Questions and Answers about
Science and Other Stuff*

Larry Scheckel

Copyright 2018, All rights reserved.

TUMBLEHOME, Inc.

Dedication

This book is dedicated to the nine Scheckel children who grew up on a farm in southwestern Wisconsin in Crawford County near Seneca: Rosemary, Edwin, Teresa, Phillip, Lawrence, Bob (deceased), Catharine, Rita, and Diane.

Contents

Chapter Three: The Science of Food and Drink

Chapter Four: Remarkable People in Science

Chapter Five : The Science of the Heavens and Earth

Chapter Six: Art, Music, Sports, and Math

Chapter Seven: Incredible Technology

Chapter Eight: At the Fringes of Science

Chapter Nine: Science Mystery and History

Chapter Ten: Chemistry and the Atom

Chapter Eleven: How the World Works

Chapter Twelve: Stuff I Always Wondered About

Foreword

Exactly a decade ago, I sat in Larry Scheckel's physics class as a student at Tomah High School. It was the beginning of my physics career, and it was about to form my life in ways I did not then understand. That class ignited my scientific curiosity. I found it extremely satisfying to be able to use physics to explain how things work in the world around me. After being accepted to college, I was offered the opportunity to add physics to my math education major. I eagerly took advantage of that opportunity, and my love for physics grew. Currently I am in my seventh year of teaching high school physics, and my journey has brought me back to that same high school physics classroom, only this time as a teacher instead of a student. Larry Scheckel started me down this path by satisfying my curiosity for how things work.

In his physics class, Larry Scheckel taught and explained physics in a way that was simple to understand. I still remember specific explanations he gave for certain phenomena, and many of them I now use when I teach those same topics. He had a way of providing simple explanations for complex situations such that anyone could understand, at any level, what was going on. As I read his explanations to the questions in this book, I am very much reminded of the way he explained topics in his classroom. His written answers are easy to read, and anyone can learn things from this book regardless of their age or science background.

Now more than ever, it is extremely critical to get people interested in science related fields. Technology continues to advance at a rapid pace, which means science related careers are changing and evolving just as quickly. We need bright young minds to continue to be interested and encouraged to pursue these careers. As a physics teacher, I am always looking for new ways to engage students in the science field. One of the best ways to do that is to use science to answer the questions about which they are curious.

In *I Wondered About That Too*, Larry Scheckel presents answers to questions students, and many other people, may have wondered about at one time or another such as; How does a black hole work? How do people record memories in their brains? How high do birds fly? How did astronauts get to the moon? What is calculus anyway?

The fact that the questions have come from children, students, and community members shows that these questions are those about which people are curious. In the same way that I found Scheckel's class satisfying my curiosity ten years ago, readers will find this book satisfying to their curiosity, interests, and desire to learn.

Oakley Moser
Tomah High School Physics Teacher

Chapter One

The Exquisite
Human Body

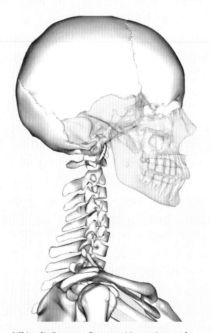

Wikimedia Commons :Rectus capitis anterior muscle

Q1: *What are people made of?*
. . . .

A lmost the entire body, about 99 percent, is made up of six elements: oxygen, carbon, hydrogen, nitrogen, calcium, and phosphorus. About one percent of the human body is composed of another five elements: potassium, sulfur, sodium, chlorine, and magnesium. All 11 elements are necessary for life. The super two are oxygen, making up 65 percent of the body, and carbon, accounting for a tad less than 19 percent.

Those elements make up our bones, muscles, tissue, fat, water, protein, carbohydrates, amino acids, hair, the works. The average 150-pound person contains a minimum of 60 trace elements. Half of these are deemed essential to a healthy human.

Yes, we also have tiny amounts of elements in our body that are not good for us. Those include cadmium, mercury, lead, arsenic, fluorine, barium, thallium, and radium.

Every one of the elements in our body, with the exception of hydrogen, was created in stars billions of years ago. As the late astrophysicist Carl Sagan reminded us, "You and I are literally made of star stuff." Those elements were forged in distant galaxies shortly after the big bang, some 13 billion years ago. The elements come from burning and exploding stars. In a weird sort of way, we are all about 13 billion years old. And here I had hopes of making it to 85 or 90, perhaps 100 at best.

We can still witness new elements being created today. "Astronomers strike gold, witness massive cosmic collision," called out a newspaper headline in August 2017. Observatories from around the world had witnessed the collision of two neutron stars that "caused the most spectacular fireworks in the universe." The Hubble Space Telescope got a snapshot of the afterglow.

Neutron stars are formed from the collapse of a massive star after a supernova explosion, if the star is massive enough to produce a black hole. The material in a neutron star, with its electrons stripped away, is so dense a teaspoon weighs a billion tons.

This particular clash happened in galaxy NGC 4993 in the constellation of Hydra, an estimated 130 million years ago, when dinosaurs roamed the earth. It took 130 million years for light, gamma rays, and gravity ripples to reach us from the constellation of Hydra.

Heavy elements were created in that distant collision. Among them were an estimated 10 billion, billion, billion dollars' worth of gold. More than enough to pay off our national debt, if only we could reach it! University of California Santa Cruz astronomer Ryan Foley announced, "We already knew that iron came from a stellar explosion, the calcium in your bones came from stars, and now we know the gold in your wedding ring came from merging neutron stars."

The first optical image from this collision showed a bright blue dot, the start of heavy element creation. After a day or two, the blue faded, becoming much fainter and redder. After three weeks, it was completely gone.

It's an incredible, yet humbling, idea that we and the entire earth originated in some far distant group of stars. Even more impressive is that we are able to figure it out. We have a brain and body to build tools and use those tools to search the universe to learn our time, position, and place in the cosmic scheme.

Q2: *How does your body keep growing after you are born?*

E very living thing, including humans, grows by cell division. Each cell has a nucleus. The nucleus divides by a process called mitosis. Each new cell receives a copy of the parent cell's genetic material.

Cells are forever dividing. More cells are being created as tissue and bones grow. Organs grow, skin grows, and everything in the body just keeps getting bigger. The human body grows constantly and steadily from birth to about age 18 or 20. You are not likely to get any taller after age 20. Of course, there is the possibility of getting w i d e r.

Bone growth determines how tall we are. The leg bones in particular grow quickly because they grow on both ends. Bones grow longer, but not much thicker. When we reach our late teens, bones stop growing.

Muscles grow along with the bones, and most growth is automatic. Some muscle growth—thickness, not length—depends on exercise. Use it or lose it!

The pelvis widens 1 inch (2.5 centimeters) between the ages of 20 and 80, even if a person watches his or her weight and keeps the same level of body fat. That means about a 3-inch (7.6-centimeter) increase in waist size. Sometimes life is not fair!

The skull continues to grow larger as we age. The forehead shifts forward a bit, making the cheekbones recede slightly.

Growth rate is not uniform for all body parts. When a baby is born, his or her head size is close to that of an adult, but the lower parts of the body are much smaller than in adults. As a child develops, the head grows very little, but the legs, arms, and torso increase greatly in size.

Genetics is the major player in growth rate. Nutrition, exercise, injury, and disease are other factors that can influence growth. In order to grow, bones need calcium and vitamins. Drink milk and skip the sugary drinks.

A leading doctor at England's Royal College of Pathologists states, "Growth of the body is really complicated, and we don't fully understand how all the bits and pieces manage to work together like a team." Life is full of mysteries.

Q3: *What color is the human brain?*

The brain has forever been referred to as gray matter. However, truth be told, the brain is fleshy pink in color. The very center of the brain is an off-white shade. The brain is very soft tissue, with the consistency of tapioca pudding.

There are three main parts to the brain: the cortex, the limbic system, and the brainstem.

The cortex handles the most advanced functions, such as thinking, making decisions, and recognizing sights, words, sounds, and sensations. We depend on the cortex for playing sports and music, and for writing.

The limbic system is involved with emotion and survival. The limbic system lets us know when we need to eat, drink water, or put on a coat when we get cold. The limbic system warns us of dangers and alerts us to threats. It is also where we experience fear, anger, aggression, pleasure, and happiness.

The brainstem connects the brain to the spinal cord, which runs down the backbone. The brainstem controls heart rate, breathing, and other vital functions. If the brainstem is badly damaged, a person can lose consciousness and lapse into a coma. The cortex needs the brainstem to keep it alive.

The brain weighs about three pounds (1.4 kilograms) and has a volume of about 1.3 quarts (1,300 cubic centimeters). Brain weight and size vary with the size of the individual. A bigger brain does not necessarily mean a smarter person.

The brain uses about 20 percent of the body's total oxygen intake. It uses oxygen to get energy by breaking down glucose and other nutrients through cellular respiration. This produces molecules of adenosine triphosphate (ATP), which are used to power many cellular processes.

If oxygen is cut off to the brain, permanent damage can occur in just four minutes. A whole slew of insults can cause the brain to malfunction. Heart attack, stroke, suffocation, drowning, or high altitude can all cut the brain's oxygen supply. Head injury or blunt trauma can also damage a healthy brain.

A stroke occurs when blood flow to a certain part of the brain is disrupted by bleeding or blockage. An aneurysm is a swelling of an artery that occurs when the artery wall is weakened. The damaged area can swell and apply undue pressure to the surrounding tissue. An aneurysm can also burst, causing a catastrophic stroke.

Tumors are growths caused by runaway cell division. Malignant, or cancerous, tumors invade surrounding tissue, causing massive damage. Benign, or noncancerous, tumors do not spread or attack other tissue, but they can apply pressure to adjacent brain tissue.

The abuse or misuse of legal and illegal drugs can damage nerve cells in the brain, leading to permanent brain damage.

Dementia is a term that describes a general decline of brain function. Dementia can manifest as memory loss, demise of thinking skills, and the inability to perform everyday activities. Alzheimer's disease accounts for about 75 percent of dementia cases.

Sometimes a medical examiner or coroner will order an autopsy of a body. The reason, of course, is to establish cause of death. As part of most autopsies, the brain is removed. The medical examiner uses an electric saw, called a Stryker saw, to make a round cut through the top of the skull. The cap of the skull bone is removed. The medical examiner employs a scalpel to cut the tissue that connects the brainstem to the spinal cord. The brain can be pulled out, stored in a solution, and made available for further examination.

The brain is a wonderful instrument. Our brain is who we are. Our body is just along for the ride, so to speak, and quite utilitarian. The brain is so complex, it has been referred to as one of the last frontiers to explore.

Q4: *How do people record memories in their brains?*

S hort-term and long-term memories are stored in the hippocampus, two small seahorse-shaped components, one on each side of the brain. The hippocampus also plays a role in spatial navigation. Damage to the hippocampus occurs early in Alzheimer's disease, leading afflicted people to become disoriented and suffer memory loss.

The first step in creating a memory is encoding. The brain has 100 billion individual cells called neurons. Those neurons send messages to one another across narrow gaps called synapses. A synapse is like a police officer directing traffic. This is where the action is. The synapse allows neurons to pass chemical and electrical signals to each other. The electrical firing of a pulse across the gap triggers a release of chemical messengers termed *neurotransmitters* that go across those synapses or spaces between cells. Each neuron has 1,000 connections to other neurons. The brain is a mighty busy place!

When a memory is created by seeing or hearing something, it must be stored. It is stored first in short-term memory. That may be as far as a memory goes. But if it is something we use over and over, such as $2 + 2 = 4$, or our social security number, or the facial features of a friend, then that important stuff is transferred to long-term memory.

Long-term memory can store a seemingly unlimited amount of information. The more that sensory input or information is repeated and used, the more likely it is to be sent to and retained in long-term memory.

It is this long-term memory that most of us think of as memory. The changes that occur as memories form in the brain are reinforced with use. If you play a piece of music over and over, the repeated firing of the associated brain cells makes it easier to repeat this process later on. You get better and better at playing music. If you stop playing for a few years, the brain starts to forget what it once knew.

There's some intriguing research that suggests that our long-term memory can be distorted without our realizing it. People can "remember" things that never really happened to them. A family story about an incident, say a weird thing that happened at a wedding, is told over and over. Somehow it makes it into your memory, even though you were not even there.

Most such memories are quite harmless. But sometimes they can have real consequences. People have been put in prison by "eyewitness" testimony, even though attorneys and judges know that such eyewitness testimony is notoriously unreliable.

A recent study had investigators ask subjects about the film footage of the United Flight 93 that crashed in Pennsylvania during the 9/11 attack. One in five "remembered" seeing the footage, even though no such footage existed. This kind of memory distortion occurs frequently, and no one is immune.

Q5: How do we digest food?
. . . .

E ntire books are devoted to digestion. It is a complex topic. But let's keep it simple. The digestive system absorbs and transports all the nutrients the body needs to live. It also gets rid of waste the body does not need.

This marvelous digestive system is a series of hollow passage-ways starting at the mouth and ending at the anus. The pancreas and liver are helpers along the way. If stretched out, the digestive tract is more than 30 feet (9 meters) long.

Food goes into the mouth, where it is chewed, and saliva se-cretes amylase to break down the food. Then the food enters a pipe called the esophagus, where muscles push it into the stom-ach. In the stomach, acids and enzymes break the food down. The stomach is coated with a mucus lining to prevent ulcers. Stomach muscles contract about every 20 seconds, stirring up the liquefied blob of food.

Next stop is the small intestine, where the food is joined by enzymes from the pancreas and bile from the liver. The small intestine absorbs water and nutrients from the food. Thousands of folds increase the surface area of the lining of the small in-testine. The surface area is about the size of a tennis court and covered by tiny projections, called villi, that pick out certain nu-trients.

What is left over travels to the large intestine, the last lap. The large intestine grabs more water, leaving behind solid waste, termed *feces*. It takes one to several days for material to run through the large intestine. The waste moves about 0.5 inch (1.3 centimeters) per hour until it is finally excreted.

It's a long, complicated process, requiring help from the liver, pancreas, and gall bladder. The liver helps break up, digest, and absorb fats. Extra bile from the liver is stored in the gall bladder to be used when it's needed. The pancreas produces juices that aid in digestion by helping bile from the liver break down proteins, fats, and carbohydrates.

With so many pipes and organs (no pun intended), there are a lot of things that can go wrong. Belching happens when too much air collects in the stomach. The main culprit is bubbly drinks. Vomiting is a protective mechanism caused by bacteria, viruses, or toxic foods irritating the stomach. Reflux occurs when stomach acids flow back up into the esophagus. Sometimes, bacteria create holes in the stomach lining. We know these painful holes as ulcers.

Other common digestive disorders are irritable bowel syndrome, excessive flatulence, constipation, and diarrhea. Digestion is quite a remarkable process. The best we can do is to treat it right by proper diet and exercise. To treat your digestive system well, avoid eating too much, do not smoke, and refrain from excessive alcohol consumption.

Q6: Why are my eyes colored?

The iris is that thin, circular, and colored structure of the eye responsible for controlling the diameter and size of the pupil. The iris governs the amount of light entering the eye and reaching the retina. Muscles attached to the iris expand and contract the pupil opening or aperture at the center of the iris. The larger the pupil, the more light can enter the eye and reach the retina. It is an automatic process.

Eye color is an inherited trait carried by as many as six genes. Color is determined by the amount, density, and type of pigment in the iris. For example, a green/blue eye color is located on chromosome 19. A brown eye and a brown/blue eye color gene are located on chromosome 15.

There are three pigment colors that combine to create the outward appearance of eye color: brown, yellow, and blue. The most common eye color is brown, and the least common is green. Babies of European ancestry are born with blue eyes. Melanin, the brown pigment that colors skin, hair, and eyes, develops later in the baby's growth. The amount and type of melanin protein is encoded in the genes. If the iris gets a lot of melanin, it will appear brown. Less melanin produces green, gray, or light brown eyes. Very little melanin means blue eyes.

Variations in eye color do have medical implications. People with lighter iris color have a higher incidence or likelihood of getting age-related macular degeneration. Color change, especially yellowing of the whites of the eye, can indicate liver disease from jaundice, cirrhosis, hepatitis, or malaria.

Retinal scans have been used for several decades to identify people. Every person has a unique pattern of blood vessels in the back of the eye. An infrared beam scans the retina, and the resulting pattern is compared to the person's scan already in the computer. Scanning the iris instead is relatively new and is unimpeded by glasses or contacts.

There are several questionnaires and surveys that purport to link eye color to personality, intelligence, athletic ability, social skills, academic achievement, or compatibility. Like those astrology columns in the newspaper, they are all nonsense.

Q7: Why does my hair keep growing?

Hair has several functions. Hair contributes to our appearance, keeps our head warm, and sends sensory information to our brain. Hair can help forensic scientists determine if a person has ingested certain poisons. Hairs can link a suspect to a crime scene or victim.

About halfway through fetal growth, a baby already has all his or her hair follicles, more than 5 million of them. That's the most they will have in their lifetime, because no new hair follicles will develop. Some people notice that hair begins to thin as a baby grows into childhood, teens, and adulthood. It makes sense. The number of hair follicles remains unchanged but the scalp is expanding as a person grows.

Hair has two parts: a follicle, which lives down inside the skin, and the shaft, which is the visible part above the skin. The hair follicle resides in layer of skin called the dermis. The dermis is just below the outer layer of skin. The epidermis is the outer layer of skin, the stuff we see and touch.

A hair follicle is a tube or tunnel segment that has several layers. The base of the follicle has a bulb-shaped structure called the papilla, where tiny blood vessels in the base nourish the hair cells. All the cells in the bulb divide in one to three days, the fastest of any cells in the body.

Two sheaths surround the follicle. Their job is to form and protect the growing hair shaft. The inner sheath follows the hair shaft. The outer sheath continues up to the sebaceous oil gland. An erector pili muscle attaches below the gland to a layer around the outer sheath. When the erector pili muscle contracts, it causes the hair to stand up and makes the sebaceous gland secrete oil.

The hair shaft itself is made of a protein called keratin, and it has three layers. Keratin is not composed of living cells. That's why it doesn't hurt when our hair is cut.

Not all hair cells operate at the same time. About a fourth of the cells are dormant. When they start working again, they push out old hairs and start making new ones. Most of us lose some hair every day, usually just by combing.

Recall those fastest of all hair-growing cells in the bulb of the follicle? Radiation and chemotherapy are designed to kill fast-growing cancer cells. Fast-growing cells in the follicle are also killed, which is why people undergoing cancer treatments often lose their hair.

Many toxic metals show up in hair samples. Iron, lead, mercury, copper, zinc, aluminum, and arsenic fall into this category. People who eat a lot of seafood may have elevated mercury levels. Smokers, including marijuana users, add a lot of cadmium to the body. Electricians and plumbers are prone to absorb copper.

Napoleon died in 1821 on the island of Saint Helena at age 51. For years, it was rumored that his British captors had poisoned him with arsenic. The official cause of death, however, was stomach cancer. A few years ago, a group of Italian scientists analyzed hair samples from three different times in Napoleon's life, as a boy in Corsica, on the day of his death, and a few days after his demise. High levels of arsenic did show up, but not higher than those from his first wife and his son, and no higher in the deathbed hairs than in his preteen years. Arsenic was used in many of the medicines of the time. No one murdered Napoleon on St. Helena.

Q8: *How does ammonia in hair dye affect the body?*

There is general agreement that all the chemicals put into our food, cleaning supplies, cosmetics, personal hygiene products, clothes, furniture, and carpet scan present challenges for our health. Yes, those artificial chemicals make our food taste better, look better, and increase shelf life. And yes, we need to use cleaning supplies, paints, and wood preservatives. The list goes on and on. But what's the cumulative harm from all those chemicals? Opinions vary widely, which is a way of saying no one knows for sure.

There are temporary hair-coloring rinses, gels, mousses, and sprays that coat the surface of the hair. They wash out in six or ten shampoos. There are also semi-permanent dyes that penetrate partway into the hair shaft. They fade and wash out in 10 to 20 shampoos. Permanent hair dyes come in two packages that are mixed together immediately before application. One package is ammonia containing the dye, and the other is hydrogen peroxide.

The pigment, or color, in our hair is stored in protein granules in the cortex of the hair beneath the scaly cuticle layer. It is the absence of that pigment that causes hair to turn gray or white. Before any permanent color can penetrate the hair shaft, the cuticle (outer layer) must be opened up so that chemicals can get where they need to be.

The job of the ammonia is to cause the hair to swell, leading the cuticle scales to separate a little so the ammonia can penetrate deeply into the hair shaft. The ammonia solution also carries the dyes or color couplers. After a while, the dye reacts with the hydrogen peroxide, also known as the developer, to produce color. This takes some time, and one must wait about a half hour or so for the color to build up.

What about safety? There have been occasional questions about hair coloring and cancer. A Harvard study found no positive association between the use of permanent hair dye and cancer. However, other studies suggest a possible link between permanent hair dyes and bladder cancer. The risk seems to apply mostly to hairstylists and barbers, because they handle and are exposed to the stuff for hours and days at a time.

Certain women may be more susceptible to bladder cancer associated with the use of permanent hair dyes than other women, based on their genetic makeup, according to researchers at the Keck School of Medicine of the University of Southern California. Some people's bodies flush out toxins better than others. The research and studies go on.

There are some generally recognized actions we can take to reduce cancer risks. Avoid processed foods with chemical additives. Avoid junk food. Choose organic fruits and vegetables. Opt for seafood known to be low in PCB and mercury, such as wild Alaska salmon and canned salmon. Use glass or ceramic containers, not plastic, to microwave foods. Men should avoid hair dyes that contain lead acetate and hormone disrupters. Avoid fumes from dry cleaners, paints, finishes, and glues. Don't smoke. Avoiding unnecessary exposure can reduce your risk.

Q9: *Why do doctors use electrical bone stimulation and how does it work?*

Bone is one of the tissues in the body that can mend itself when injured. Fractured bones go through a natural healing process that allows new bone tissue to grow across the gap. First, the gap fills with a blood clot called a fracture hematoma, then with bone-forming cells. Finally, the cells calcify into bone.

A break will usually repair itself into a solid union within a few months. But that doesn't always happen. At times, the normal process of bone calcification does not take place, as scar tissue and cartilage fill the gap where new bone was expected to grow.

Various technologies exist to stimulate bone growth. One is ultrasound, and another is electrical bone stimulation. The most common unit of electrical stimulation uses *capacitive coupling* technology. This technology employs a stimulator unit with two light weight electrodes placed on either side of the bone break or bone fracture. A tiny electrical current passes between the electrodes. The patient cannot feel the current.

Electrical stimulation causes bone cells to proliferate. The idea is to increase the flow of calcium ions into osteoblasts, the cells that deposit new bone. Electrical stimulation has been used successfully on breaks and fractures of the humerus (bone from the elbow to shoulder), the ulna and radius (bones from the elbow to hand), the femur (bone from the hip to knee), and the tibia and fibula (bones from the ankle to knee).

Electrical stimulation is especially useful on scaphoid fractures. The scaphoid bone is one of eight small bones that make up the wrist. These eight bones are in two rows, but the scaphoid bone links the two rows together, putting it at high risk for injury. Fractures of the scaphoid occur when a person falls on an outstretched hand. This injury is common among athletes.

Another type of unit uses pulsed electromagnetic fields. A coil is incorporated into the cast or placed directly on the skin over the fracture site. The unit can be programmed to the patient's needs. A small electrical current travels to the treatment coil and produces a pulsating electromagnetic field around the fracture. The system is very safe, the patient feels nothing, and no surgery is required. There are no known risks or side effects. About 10 hours is the recommended time each day, and the unit can be used while the patient is sleeping.

Electrical stimulation can also be used for spinal bone fusion. Spinal bone fusion describes a surgical procedure designed to eliminate motion across a spinal segment. The technique involves placing a bone graft across the spinal segments.

Two types of bone stimulators can be employed in spinal bone fusion. One device can be implanted during surgery. It consists of a battery pack that provides direct current to four electrodes. The battery pack is implanted just below the skin.

The second stimulator uses a corset-like device that has magnetic coils implanted in it. The patient wears it while sleeping. Pulsating electromagnetic energy induces weak electrical current in the underlying tissue.

Smoking cigarettes has a significant effect on bone healing. Smoking causes blood vessels to constrict about 25 percent of their normal diameter. Nutrients, minerals, and oxygen levels are reduced. Smokers can take more than two months longer for their bones to heal compared to nonsmokers.

Q10: If I drink gallons of Coke, how long will it take to rot my teeth?

I asked my dentist, Dr. Scott Nicol, this question and he responded, "Not long." This is not only because of the sugar, but also because Coke makers add phosphoric acid to the cola ingredients. That's the same acid dentists use for etching the enamel prior to repairing a chipped tooth.

Phosphoric acid corrodes and dissolves the calcium out of the tooth enamel, leaving a softened matrix where bacteria can enter the teeth and cause wholesale destruction. Sugar feeds the bacteria that form plaque, and the bacteria then release acid that hollows out cavities within the teeth. It's a double whammy.

Drinking sugar-free sodas is not the answer. The phosphoric acid is still in there. Bottlers and canners add phosphoric acid to give the cola a tangy taste. Phosphoric acid is mass-produced and much cheaper than ginger or citric acids obtained from lemons or limes.

One dentist on the Internet states that "every time you drink a soda you get twenty seconds of acid attack on your teeth, which in time will eat away at your enamel and cause a cavity. If you must have your daily dose, it is best to drink it all at once and not sip on it throughout the day. Also, it's best to brush after consuming your soda, if possible. If not, try to swish with some water."

Soda contents include high-fructose corn syrup, additive dye, acid, and caffeine. An average can of soda has 12 teaspoons (59 milliliters) of sugar and 40 to 48 milligrams of phosphoric acid. Mountain Dew has 55 milligrams of caffeine. A cup of coffee has between 75 and 150 milligrams of caffeine.

Even fruit juice can be bad for teeth. Dr. Nicol says dentists are seeing more cases of "bottle rot." Some young parents put sweetened juices in sippy cups. Those juices are loaded with sugar, and babies typically don't get their teeth brushed on a regular basis.

Soft drink consumption has leveled off and slightly decreased in the past few years. However, more than half of children and teens drink at least one soda per day. Some drink four or five cans per day. The size of soft drinks has also risen. In the 1950s, a 6.5-ounce (0.2 liter) bottle of soda was popular. Now the sizes are 12 ounces (0.4 liter), and there are some big gulps of up to 30 and 40 ounces (0.9 and 1.2 liters) and more.

Soft drinks have replaced milk in the diets of many American children as well as adults. School purchases reflect such trends. In recent years, school districts decreased the amounts of milk they bought by nearly 30 percent and increased their purchases of carbonated soft drinks.

Studies show the teenage girls require 1,300 milligrams of calcium per day and are getting only 800 milligrams. Calcium is needed for bone development and growth up to age 18. Lack of calcium after that may lead to later osteoporosis and broken bones.

Teenage boys drink more soda than girls. Health risks for boys include diabetes, kidney stones, obesity, osteoporosis, and tooth destruction. In 88 separate studies, there was a strong association between soft drink consumption and body weight. In response to this information, some schools have banned soft drinks.

Q11: Do mercury-based vaccines cause autism?

T he short answer is NO. Let me explain.

The question concerns thimerosal, a mercury-based preservative used to prevent contamination of multidose vials of vaccine, especially the measles, mumps, and rubella (MMR) vaccine. At one point, thimerosal was added in the manufacturing process to stop growth of bacteria and fungi.

The medical profession is satisfied that thimerosal is safe, but there are a few skeptics. They point to cases where children first showed autism symptoms sometime after receiving the MMR vaccine. As a result, thimerosal has been removed from routine childhood vaccines.

I would like to discuss the difference between causation and correlation by using a case study of another drug, Bendectin, approved by the FDA and put on the market in 1956.

For twenty-plus years, Bendectin was prescribed for women as a treatment for morning sickness and its accompanying nausea and vomiting during pregnancy. In late 1979, the *National Enquirer* published a story that told of thousands of women who had taken Bendectin and then given birth to babies with birth defects.

The manufacturer, Merrell, sought to reassure people that the drug was safe, that extensive research and testing had been carried out, and that there was no connection between birth defects and Bendectin use.

Well, you know what's going to happen. Call in the lawyers. Trials, courts, and juries across the country. Some found Bendectin to be bad stuff, and some found Bendectin to be blameless.

In mid-1984, nearly 1,000 cases were combined into a big trial in Cincinnati. Even though Merrell was convinced that Bendectin was safe, it agreed to pay out $120 million before the trial even started. Ah, but the lawyers for the plaintiffs, the ones suing, decided they could get more money. So the trial went ahead.

The presiding judge made several stipulations. First, the trial would revolve around whether Bendectin caused birth defects, and the decision would be based on science, not sympathy. To that end, children with visible handicaps were not allowed in the courtroom. The use of the emotionally charged word *thalidomide* (an earlier drug that actually *had* caused birth defects) was forbidden.

If the jury found that Bendectin did cause birth defects, the trial would move to the next two stages, to determine which children were harmed and what compensation was due them and their families.

It was a long trial, but it took the jury only five hours to find that Bendectin did not cause birth defects. How could that be? If these 1,000 women all took Bendectin, and all 1,000 had children with birth defects, why did the jury say that Bendectin wasn't the cause?

We need to look at the bigger picture. More than 30 million women had taken Bendectin. The overwhelming majority of their children were born without birth defects. But every year, with or without Bendectin, there are more than 100,000 children born in the United States with some kind of birth defect. It's not hard to understand that thousands of children with birth defects were born to women who took Bendectin, even if the drug was harmless.

It is most important not to confuse causation with correlation. What if we found 1,000 women who ate pancakes during their pregnancy, and who subsequently had kids with birth defects? Should we conclude that pancakes caused the birth defects?

The real stunner here is that Merrell pulled the drug from the market. Not because it was dangerous, but because it was too expensive to defend against lawsuits. During the five-year period from 1980 to 1985 in which Bendectin use declined and stopped altogether, birth defect rates remained constant, and hospitalizations for morning sickness cases doubled.

Will drug companies, fearing lawsuits, be reluctant to do research or provide drugs that might help pregnant women? Morning sickness is a serious malady. Untreated nausea can be harmful to both mother and fetus, causing malnutrition. Charlotte Brontë, the author of the novel *Jane Eyre*, died of morning sickness in 1855. She was 38.

Returning to the saga of autism and thimerosal. In 1988, a British surgeon and medical researcher, Dr. Andrew Wakefield, got an article published in the prestigious medical journal *Lancet* claiming a relationship between the MMR vaccine and autism.

Lancet retracted the article two years later, and the medical profession found Wakefield's research to be fraudulent and self-serving, meaning he was in it for the money. In fact, Dr. Wakefield lost his British medical license because of his unethical research on patients.

A similar story explains why we no longer have a vaccine for Lyme disease. The pharmaceutical company GlaxoSmithKline developed LYMErix. It was approved by the FDA and put on the market in 1998. A few people came forward to complain of chronic arthritis reactions to the vaccine, namely 59 out of 1.4 million doses. The FDA reviewed LYMErix a second time and found the rate of new arthritis cases was no greater than among people who did not receive the vaccine.

But loud voices get publicity, and a small but vocal Lyme disease counterculture developed. Fearing class action lawsuits and declining sales, GlaxoSmithKline pulled the vaccine from the market in 2002. Lyme disease continues to increase and now has spread into Canada.

Q12: *Why do I feel pain?*

Pain is a signal that something has gone haywire with our body. Our body is damaged, and something may need to be done. Pain is a defense mechanism. It can typically stop us from continuing to do whatever caused the pain. No matter how much we hate pain, it does play an important role. Without pain, we wouldn't be able to sense an injury. We might be in danger of hurting ourselves even more, for example by walking on glass or skiing on a broken leg.

Pain is a warning signal that we are in danger and we need to change our course of action. If we touch a live wire, the pain of the shock tells us to move away. If we hold a hot pan, pain tells us to drop it or set it down quickly.

The pain signal also triggers the "flight or fight syndrome." Our body is put on alert or alarm status. The muscles receive a greater supply of blood, the heart rate increases, breathing picks up, and we get ready to stand and fight or to flee from danger.

The spinal cord is the main route for pain messaged to the brain. When we hurt ourselves, such as by stubbing a toe, we activate pain receptors, which are single purpose nerve fibers. Their function is to set off the alarm.

The pain receptors send impulses through the nerve into the spinal cord, where the signals make their way to the brain. The impulses move through our bodies at a rate of up to 30 meters (almost 100 feet) per second. When a pain signal reaches the brain, it goes directly to the thalamus, and from there is dispatched to areas for interpretation. The thalamus not only acts as the messenger, but also initiates an emotional response, such as anger, frustration, crying, or as sometimes in my case, swearing.

There are two distinct types of pain, acute and chronic. Acute pain refers to pain newly acquired that often needs immediate action. Examples are a fall from a ladder, striking a finger instead of a nail with a hammer, breaking an arm, or being hit by a baseball. Chronic pain is associated with an old injury, the wear and tear of old age, or a condition brought on by maladies such as fibromyalgia or arthritis. Chronic pain nags at a person for a long time and can make us depressed or inactive.

English biologist Richard Dawkins claims that "pain is a remarkably complex and multifaceted process." MRI scans show an abnormal amount of stimulation in the brains of chronic pain sufferers. These folks perceive and feel pain differently and more intensely. Their central nervous system has altered to become more sensitive to pain. Sometimes, to them, even a slight touch may feel painful.

There are other kinds of pain. Neuropathic pain refers to sensations of tingling, electrical shocks, or pins and needles. It's the kind of pain you feel when you hit your funny bone.

Phantom pain is pain felt in a body part that has been amputated, such as an arm or leg. For some reason, nerve endings to this missing part, which is no longer sending true signals to the brain, can send pain signals instead.

There is no consensus on measuring pain. There are more than 20 different scales that are utilized in varying venues and jurisdictions. Many health-care providers use a numeric rating scale, sometimes with matching pictures. They ask their patients to rate their pain from 1 to 10, with 10 being the most excruciating pain they can imagine.

Many people who must deal with chronic pain have found various coping strategies, including distraction, regular relaxation, exercise, being assertive and clear about their needs, pacing their activities, finding things that give pleasure, and challenging negative thoughts. Medication can sometimes help, but it is important to avoid long-term use of powerful opioid medications, which can lead to addiction.

The addiction to opioids, or prescription painkillers, has been the leading health news story for the past several years. Death due to opioid addiction is so widespread it is believed to be the biggest factor in a decline in overall US life expectancy.

Robert Anderson, a statistician at the Centers for Disease Control and Prevention stated, "We could see more than two years of declining life expectancy in a row, which we haven't seen since the influenza pandemic of 1918." In 2016, the last year of released numbers, more than 63,600 Americans, many in young adulthood or middle age, died from opioid overdose.

Chapter Two

All the Plants and Animals

Q13: Do fish drink water?
. . . .

F reshwater fish do not drink water through their mouths, but they do absorb water through their gills and skin. Saltwater fish actively drink seawater right through their mouths.

Start with freshwater fish, the kind we find in Lake Tomah, up on the cranberry marshes, and in the Wisconsin and Mississippi Rivers. The salt concentration in the cells of freshwater fish is higher than the surrounding water. Thus, by osmosis, fish absorb water through their skin. Osmosis is the movement of a liquid through a membrane from the side with higher water concentration (less salt) to the side with lower water concentration (more salt). Freshwater fish urinate profusely to prevent their tissue from becoming too watery. If freshwater fish drank water, they would bloat up like balloons.

Saltwater fish have a concentration of salt in their cells that is lower than the surrounding seawater. They need to drink large amounts of water just to stay hydrated. These fish must drink water to replace what they lose by osmosis, as water moves from their bodies to the saltier water surrounding them. To get rid of the extra salt they drink in, they must actively pump salt, especially chlorine, out of their bodies. The salt exits through cells at the base of the gills. Saltwater fish urinate very little. If saltwater fish didn't drink water, they would shrivel up.

A few fish manage a wide range of saltiness. Salmon live in both saltwater and freshwater. Salmon are born in freshwater and then they move out to ocean saltwater. They drink saltwater through their mouth, and their gills filter out the salt.

When the salmon return to freshwater rivers and streams to spawn, they start to absorb water through their skin and into their cells by osmosis. Quite a remarkable ability and adaptation!

Q14: *How do animals survive very cold winters?*

Mammals such as bears stay warm by growing thick fur. They also become partially dormant, or hibernate, in winter. Groundhogs burrow down into the ground and sleep all winter. Foxes, chipmunks, and moles also dig deep into the ground. Reptiles go to lower places, and amphibians seek deeper water.

Torpidity is the controlled reduction of body metabolism, meaning low oxygen use and lowered body temperature. Hibernation is the most extreme form of torpidity, but the animal kingdom practices a wide array of dormancies. Some animals undergo daily states of torpidity in response to lack of food. Examples include squirrels and rabbits.

Some birds flee the North and wisely head south for the winter months, where they encounter warmer weather and a plentiful food supply. Geese, ducks, cranes, and robins all point their beaks southward come September and October. Hummingbirds fly all the way across the Gulf of Mexico. The monarch butterfly migrates to Mexico.

Those birds that stay in our North Country must keep warm by pumping more blood, using a faster heart rate. They use their feathers to trap warm air against their skin. They eat all the time to maintain a sufficiently high body temperature. They stay out of the wind and avoid getting wet. They also roost together, sharing body heat.

Some animals eat like mad in the summer and store up fat for the long winter. Fat is a good insulator. An insulator is anything that does not let heat through. Otters and mink, for example, grow thick layers of insulating fat.

There are very few small animals in the Arctic. Small animals have a lot more surface area compared to their weight and volume. This means that small animals such as mice lose much more of their body heat through their skin than large animals. Mice and hummingbirds must eat constantly just to stay alive.

You might want to try this little experiment. Spoon 1 cup (237 milliliters) of lard or shortening into a zippered storage bag. Turn a second zippered storage bag inside out and put it inside the shortening bag. Zip the two bags together so the first bag is sealed to the second bag. Put one hand inside the bag that has the shortening. Now put each hand in a bowl of ice water. The hand in the insulating fat stays warm while the unprotected hand suffers!

Q15: Do koala bears only live in Australia?
. . . .

Yes, Australia is the only country where koala bears live in the wild. Outside of Australia, you can find them only in zoos.

Koala bears live in eucalyptus trees, where they eat the leaves at night and sleep during the day. They sleep 75 percent of the time, sitting in the forks of the trees. The long sleep periods are necessary to digest their eucalyptus leaf diet. Eucalyptus leaves are 50 percent water. As a result, koala bears do not drink water unless there is a severe drought.

Koalas get up and start moving right after sunset. They can be heard barking at other koalas. The cute and cuddly koalas live 10 to 12 years on average. Typical adults are 30 inches (76 centimeters) in length and weigh about 15 pounds (6.8 kilograms). As in most mammals, the male is a bit larger than the female. The ear tips sport long white hairs.

Koala bears are a protected species these days, but that was not always the case. John Price, a servant of Tasmania's governor, was the first European to record koalas in 1798. The koala fur is thick and soft and pleasant to the touch, so it was understandable that millions were shot for their pelts. They were hunted to near extinction by 1930. Now that they are protected, they can no longer be hunted. Today their greatest foes are cars, dogs, and loss of habitat due to farming. Large birds also prey on koala bears.

Koalas have a societal structure and need to be around other koalas. If one dies, others will avoid the area of the deceased for about a year, until the scent markings and scratches on trees have disappeared. Koalas breed once a year. A baby koala, called a joey, is hairless, 1 inch (2.5 centimeters) long, and blind. It weighs about 1 gram, which is the weight of a dollar bill or a paperclip.

Koala bears are marsupials. Marsupial mothers carry their young in a frontal pouch. Other common marsupials are kangaroos, possums, wallabies, and wombats. Using its sense of smell, the newborn joey climbs into its mother's pouch. The small creature nurses in the pouch for about six months. The joey or cub stays with the mother for about a year. Twins are rare, and a mother koala bear will produce five or six youngsters in her lifetime.

It is quite amazing how the koala bear adapts to the cold, utilizing some of the same techniques as humans. They have very little insulating fat. They conserve heat by reducing blood flow to the extremities. They shiver, so that rapid contractions of muscles create heat. When it gets too hot, on the other hand, they increase respiration rates. This increases evaporation in the airways to regulate body temperature.

Q16: Why do lions roar?
· ·

L ions roar to communicate. Most all animals will bark, tweet, sing, quack, snort, hum, chirp, squeal, meow, howl, wail, or warble, making sounds to signal their own kind and others in their area. The male lion roars in the evening to let other animals know he is guarding his territory. His main task in lion life is to protect his pride, his lady friends and children, if you will. *Keep your distance and leave me in peace*, is his message. If he didn't roar, he would have to get up and check out anything that stirred in the night.

Zookeepers know that each lion has a different voice, or sound, and they can tell which lion is "talking." The mama lion uses a quieter, gentler roar when she calls her cubs.

Lions also roar when hunting their prey. They silently creep up on their intended meal, and when posed to strike, let out a roar that confuses and terrorizes their victim. That lion roar can be quite loud, as much as 115 decibels at 3 feet (0.9 meters). That's louder than a jackhammer, loud enough to be heard 2 miles (3.2 kilometers) away.

What's the difference between a lion and a tiger? Tigers are bigger than lions. The biggest tiger is the Siberian tiger. The tiger has stripes against an orange background coat, whereas a lion's fur is yellowish. Male lions sport a mane, but the female's neck is bare. The lion's roar is louder, but the tiger has a deeper, more bass, growl. The lion has habitat in Africa and India. The tiger can be found in the Indian subcontinent.

Lions hunt in packs, with the female lions doing the heavy lifting. They feast primarily on wildebeest (a type of antelope) and zebra. Male lions prefer just to eat, not hunt. Tigers hunt alone. Both lions and tigers kill by strangulation, clamping down on the neck of their prey until it is dead.

The Big Four cats are the tiger, lion, jaguar, and leopard. They are the cats that roar. People sometimes want to include the cougar, cheetah, and snow leopard. All seven of these cats are meat eaters and apex predators. Apex predators reign atop the food chain, having no natural predators of their own.

Q17: *Which type of snake is deadliest?*

This is an excellent question, but not a simple one. It's like asking "Who was the best baseball player ever?" or "Who was the best president we've ever had?" There are many different ways to arrive at an answer. People will come up with different answers and rankings.

For the world's deadliest snakes, one must look at several criteria. Those might include the toxicity of the venom, the number of snakebite deaths per year, the size of the adult, the amount of venom per bite, and the aggressive nature of the snake.

The black mamba would be on everyone's top 10 list. This "bad boy" snake is found in all African countries except the desert countries of the North. The black mamba averages more than 8 feet (2.4 meters) in length and can travel up to 12 miles (19 kilometers) per hour. The black mamba is olive green in color, but the inside of its mouth is black, hence its name. This snake is very territorial, does not like intruders, and will strike or bite repeatedly, up to 12 times in a row. When threatened or cornered, the black mamba will hiss, flatten its neck, and display its inky mouth and two large fangs. It can rear up to one third of its body from the ground, a distance of up to 4 feet (1.2 meters).

Most snake poisons are hemotoxic and travel slowly through the bloodstream. This allows time for a tourniquet to isolate the poison, or to get treatment by using a snakebite kit.

The black mamba poison is neurotoxic. It rushes right to the nerves, attacks the central nervous system, and shuts down major organs. A single bite from a black mamba is enough to kill ten adults. A victim will be comatose in an hour and dead in six hours. You do not want a black mamba for a pet!

The inland taipan, sometimes called the fierce snake, is native to Australia's central arid areas. Its venom is the most toxic known. A single bite could kill 100 people. Fortunately, this "fierce snake" is rather timid and will strike only if provoked. These snakes live in holes and feed on mice and rats.

Wisconsin has 21 species of snakes, but only two are venomous, the eastern Massasauga rattlesnake and the timber rattlesnake. The Massasauga rattlesnake is on the endangered list, and the timber rattlesnake is on the protected wild animal list. It is illegal to hunt or own either snake. The timber rattler lives mostly along the rocky bluffs of the Mississippi and Wisconsin Rivers. The Massasauga, a Chippewa name meaning "great river mouth," favors wetlands and riverbeds and is found from Ontario, Canada, to Southwest Arizona.

When I was a kid growing up in rural Crawford County, Wisconsin, there was a bounty on rattlesnakes, gophers, and moles. Rattlesnake tails fetched as much as five dollars. Mole feet were a quarter and gopher tails earned a nickel. Most of the bounties were taken off in the mid-1970s.

Q18: How high do birds fly?

According to the *Guinness Book of Records*, the highest recorded flight for a bird was in November 1973 when a vulture collided with a jet airliner over the Ivory Coast in Africa. The passenger jet was cruising at 37,000 feet (11,278 meters) when a Ruppell's griffon vulture, with a 10-foot (3-meter) wingspan, was sucked into one of the jet engines. The Smithsonian National Museum of Natural History identified the bird by examining the feathers. The jet landed safely.

The highest recorded altitude for a bird in the United States was a mallard duck that collided with a commercial jet over Elko, Nevada, in July 1963. The duck and plane were flying at 21,000 feet (6,400meters). The plane landed safely.

Most migrating birds fly at less than 1,000 feet (305 meters) above the ground. Small songbirds typically are seen between 500 feet (152 meters) and 2,000 feet (610 meters). Some go up to 15,000 feet (4,600 meters) to catch favorable winds.

The birds that fly the highest on a regular basis are the migratory bar-headed geese that fly over the Himalayan Mountains between Tibet and India. They have been spotted soaring over the top of Mount Everest, which is a bit more than 29,000 feet (8,800 meters). Bar-headed geese have a special type of hemoglobin that absorbs oxygen very quickly at high altitudes. They are endowed with capillaries that go deep within their muscles to take oxygen right to the muscle fiber.

Scientists believe the less dense air at high altitudes poses a problem for most birds. The lighter air at high altitudes gives birds less lift. It is to their advantage to fly low. The air pressure difference between the cavities in the head of the bird and the outside pressure can also cause the bird discomfort. The same thing happens to people when airliners ascend or descend at a high rate of speed.

Q19: Do migrating birds get jet lag?
. . . .

No, birds don't seem to be bothered by jet lag. Jet lag is caused by passing rapidly through time zones. Birds tend to fly between breeding grounds in the North and wintering grounds in the South, most often staying in the same time zone. And if they do cross time zones, they might take several days, if not weeks, to do so.

One could speculate that birds are immune to jet lag because they don't have to put up with lost luggage, extra charges for suitcases, narrow seats, seats that recline into your chest, airline food, airport delays, canceled flights, crying babies in the seats ahead and behind, and overhead bins that are so full they may burst open and conk you on the head.

Birds don't fly from Chicago to Beijing or New York to Sydney in one day. They don't really stretch their physical limits unless they are forced to, such as flying over a large body of water. If birds get tired, they land, feed, rest, and continue the next day.

Going east is harder on the body than traveling west. Moving east means the body clock must be advanced. That's harder than going west, where the time zones dictate a slower advance of the body clock. Moving east across seven or more time zones, such as flying from Chicago to Rome, or Minneapolis to Oslo, causes the most problems for American travelers. The most common trouble is getting to sleep if going east and waking up too early if flying west. Difficulties may include interrupted sleep, frequently waking during the night, fatigue, headaches, irritability, and digestion problems.

The medical profession even has a medical term for jet lag, called *circadian dysrhythmia*. The body's clock, or circadian rhythm, gets out of step as it experiences patterns of daylight and darkness different from those to which it has been accustomed. We all have a natural pattern of eating, sleeping, and working, and that steady pattern is disturbed.

Is there a cure for jet lag? Management of light is a trick used by frequent flyers such as professional athletes, business people, and diplomats. They often wear sleep glasses that cover the eyes. These can help them adjust their circadian rhythm closer to the 24-hour cycle of their destination. Adjusting eating times and amounts and exercise routines are helpful to many. Fortunately, jet lag only lasts a few days, at most.

But back to the birds. Around 2,000 bird species migrate, out of a total of 10,000 bird species. Most fly in flocks, and larger birds, such as geese, travel in the familiar V formation to conserve energy by taking advantage of the upwash vortex created by the wings of the bird in front and off to the side.

The Arctic tern migrates one of the longest distances, flying from its Arctic breeding grounds in the Far North to its Antarctic nonbreeding places in the Far South. The Arctic tern sees two summers a year and more daylight than any other bird.

Hummingbirds fly very large distances, usually at night. They land in the morning, eat and rest for a few days, then continue. They fly at night to avoid predators and prevent overheating by taking advantage of the cooler air.

The famous song "When the Swallows Come Back to Capistrano" celebrates the cliff swallows that return each year to the old Spanish mission at San Juan Capistrano, just south of Los Angeles. These mud-nest builders winter in Argentina and fly 6,000 miles (9,700 kilometers) to return to the mission, arriving each year on March 19, Saint Joseph's Day. They fly back south to Argentina leaving on October 23, Saint John of Capistrano's Day.

Do visit the great stone church at San Juan, see the swallows and their mud nests. It is the oldest building in California, erected in 1782. With beautiful grounds and many artifacts, it is a most peaceful place.

Bad bird migration joke:

Two birds migrating south are flying over Camp Randall stadium at University of Wisconsin–Madison. The football contest below is between the Badgers and the Ohio State Buckeyes. The one bird says, "Who do you think is going to win that game down there?" His aviating buddy, with a mischievous wink, replies, "Well, I don't know, but I just put everything I had on the Buckeyes."

Q20: *Why do bees make honey?*

Bees make honey to prepare for winter. Honey is the food bees rely on when the weather turns cold. Bees live in highly socialized communities where each bee has its own job. The worker bees (all female) go from flower to flower gathering the nectar. A single bee may visit as many as 1,000 flowers. Her load arriving back at the hive is about half her weight. Very impressive!

The nectar does not go into the bee's stomach. It is collected in a special storage sac called the honey crop. As the worker bee swallows the nectar, she adds enzymes to it from special glands. This starts the process of breaking down the complex sucrose into simpler sugars—glucose and fructose.

When the worker bee gets to the hive, she passes the nectar to a hive bee (also females) that swallows it again, adding more enzymes. The hive bee puts the nectar into a honeycomb cell.

When it first enters the hive, the honey contains too much water. If left untreated, the honey would ferment and spoil. The hive bees fan the stored honey with their wings and cause much of the water to evaporate away. With the aid of air movement and heat, the water turns from a liquid to a vapor. Bees figure that 18 percent water is about right. When the bees somehow decide the honey is ready, they cover the cell with wax to seal it. That's when the beekeeper comes along and steals the honey.

The flowers also get something out of this deal. Plants use nectar as a way of attracting bees. As bees gather nectar, they also transfer pollen grains from one flower to another, thus pollinating other flowers.

Honey is a very stable food source. It resists bacteria, fungi, mold, and a host of other microbes. Honey can be stored for years without refrigeration. Ancient honey has even been found in the pyramids.

Worker bees are not able to reproduce. They live only six weeks in the summer and four to nine months in winter. They literally work themselves to death. A hive will have about 50,000 worker bees in the busy season. They can sting once, but then they die.

The hive does have some male bees, called drones. They come from eggs that have not been fertilized. The word *drone* is derived from an old English word *dran*, which literally means "idler" or "lazy worker." The drone can't sting. The sole job of the drone is to mate with the queen bee. The drone has a barbed sex organ. After mating, the drone dies. Come winter, remaining drones are of no use and are expelled from the hive.

If you choose to be a bee, be a queen. There is only one queen bee per hive. Queen bees live from three to five years. The queen mates once with several drone bees and remains fertile for life. She lays about 1,500 eggs per day. Fertilized eggs become female worker bees and unfertilized eggs become the male drone bees.

When the queen dies, the other bees make a new queen by selecting a young larva and feeding it a special royal jelly. This milky substance, made from digested pollen and nectar, is loaded with vitamin B. Long live the queen!

Q21: *What makes a bee buzz?*

A bee's wings create that buzzing sound. The size of a flying insect determines the number of beats per second and hence the pitch of the sound. Small wings can't push as much air as big wings, so they must beat faster. A mosquito has very small wings and beats them between 400 to 500 times a second. The sound they make is more of a whine than a buzz. A honeybee has medium-sized wings and flaps them around 250 times a second. They make that familiar buzz. A butterfly has quite large wings and beats them around six times per second. That speed is so low and slow that the sound is in the infrasonic range and we don't hear it.

Bee buzz tone may change. Pitch, tone, and frequency are all pretty much the same, namely, the number of vibrations per second. If a bee's nest is disturbed, or if the bees are attacked and defending themselves from enemy predators, the buzz pitch goes way up. Similarly, if bees are disrupted during foraging, buzz frequency rises. If there is a conflict in the hive with the queen bee, the buzz tone really goes up.

Buzz tone changes when the bee is out pollinating some, but not all, flowers. These flowers release their pollen only when shaken. Bumblebees shake the anthers, or male parts, of the flower, where the pollen is stored, by placing the upper part of their body (thorax) close to the anther. Then they vibrate their flight muscles very fast to shake loose the pollen. It produces a noticeably higher pitch.

Another high-pitched sound, called piping, is made by bees just prior to swarming, or when a hive is disturbed. Most researchers claim piping comes from the queen bee. Other bee experts say that piping starts with a small group of forager bees, or nest-site scouts, and they get the rest of the hive all riled up.

Honeybee queens make different piping sounds during different periods of development.

Piping is more common when there is potentially more than one queen in a hive. It is thought that the new queen is ready to fight for the right to be the one-and-only queen. Sort of a queen-fight. Hearing the sound, the worker bees try keeping the candidate queens separate so that help is available if an emergency knocks one queen off and they need a new queen.

A mated queen will pipe when released into a colony. That signals that she is ready to take over, and it would be a good idea if all the other bees "pipe down" and obey. The piping pitch is said to be about a G sharp or A flat (same note) on the musical scale. Queens also do quacking, a series of short pulses.

Pollination is plant reproduction. It is the transfer of pollen from the anther to the female part of a flower, called the stigma. When pollen meets the stigma, a plant's nut, seed, or fruit begins to form. We know that bees are important for pollinating garden crops grown for their fruits, such as tomatoes, watermelon, and cantaloupes. They also fertilize vegetable crops such as cucumbers, squash, pumpkins, asparagus, and broccoli.

In the orchard, we count on pollination for apples and cherries. Some field crops, such as alfalfa and clover, also rely on the bee. A biggie in our area of Wisconsin is the cranberry. Growers rent beehives from Texas and Oklahoma, and we see the hives populating the dikes beside the marshes.

In the past few years, beekeepers have noticed many of their hives failing. There is a special name for it: Colony Collapse Disorder (CCD). For some reason, nearly all the worker bees abandon a hive, leaving behind the queen and larvae, which don't survive without them. Beekeepers have lost as many as one third of their hives to CCD per year.

Several possible causes of CCD have been proposed. A mite infestation may have decimated some hives. Pesticides may also be a culprit. Many corn, soybean, canola, and sunflower seeds are pesticide-coated. The chemicals travel through the plants and kill insects that munch on the roots and leaves. Some of these neurotoxins have been blamed for killing both bees and butterflies.

Monoculture, the growing of only one type of crop over a large area, may also harm bees by depriving them of a varied diet. You can easily imagine that bees need plants that are flowering at different times to sustain them throughout the year. Other hypotheses refer to changes in climate or infection with viruses.

Research on CCD continues. Luckily, in the past few years, the number of honeybee colonies has been growing worldwide. That's the buzz on bees.

Q22: *Why do mosquitoes come out at night?*

Those pesky critters are crepuscular feeders. *Crepuscular* is from a Latin word meaning "twilight." So mosquitoes like their meals at dawn and dusk. However, out of 3,000 known species of mosquitoes, there are a few that will bite any time of day.

Mosquitoes are very lightweight and spindly and find it hard to maneuver in strong winds. Light breezes can help them scout out blood hosts by finding carbon dioxide sources, like humans. Strong winds blow the smells and the mosquitoes around.

Only the female mosquito will bite, which means she draws blood. She wants a blood meal to help grow her eggs. She can lay between 100 and 300 eggs at a time and will average between 1,000 and 3,000 offspring in her lifetime.

Mosquitoes seek warmth but do not like hot, dry conditions. They can easily overheat and desiccate, or dry up, in direct sunlight. They like quiet, calm, warm, and moist places.

Mosquitoes have been around for an estimated 100 million years. Not only are they hunters of prey, but they have evolved ways to avoid predators. Dusk is the time that birds are going to sleep. Bats are just waking up and starting to move out to hunt. Mosquitoes are most active at a time when their enemies are inactive.

Mosquitoes have rather poor eyesight. At 50 feet (15 meters), they can't distinguish between a person and an Allis-Chalmers tractor. Mosquitoes locate their target by heat, scent, and finally eyesight. At 100 feet (31 meters) away, they can sense a human being by the carbon dioxide we exhale. At the 10-foot (3-meter) distance, the irritating pests employ very sensitive thermal receptors on the tips of their antennas to locate blood near the surface of the skin. If the humidity is high, the range of their receptors increases threefold.

The diseases that mosquitoes carry include malaria, yellow fever, dengue fever, and encephalitis. Mosquitoes transmit heart worms to cats and dogs.

Mosquitoes breed in standing water, so obviously getting rid of these sources reduces the population. Water stands in places like old tires, tree holes, rain gutters, unattended bird baths, and any stagnant pool of water. Wetland areas are problematic. We can't just drain them, because ecosystems need wetlands for water storage.

DEET seems to be the leading anti-mosquito chemical. It is found in most repellants. Bug zappers do not kill many mosquitoes. Instead, they kill beneficial insects such as moths and butterflies, which pollinate flowers.

Q23: *How does a seed know which way to grow?*
· ·

A plant response that involves a specific movement is called *tropism*, from the Greek word meaning "to turn." Any factor that brings forth such a response is called a stimulus.

Tests done way back in 1806 confirmed that gravity was the primary cause of plants growing in the correct direction. The tests showed that moisture was not the cause. Plant shoots kept in the dark still grew up and roots grew down, so light was not the primary reason either.

How did researchers prove that gravity was the factor? Around 200 years ago, British scientist Thomas Knight put seedlings in a rotating wheel, so they "felt" an artificial gravity-like pull of centrifugal force. The plant roots grew downward at a 45-degree angle. The 45-degree angle was the result of both centrifugal force and gravity.

The tropism responsible for plants growing in the correct direction is geotropism, a response to gravity. NASA uses the term *gravitropism*.

Thigmotropism is a response to touch. It causes vines to twine around an object. Think of the climbing plants and ivy you see up the sides of buildings and old windmills out in the country.

Cells that are touched produce auxin, a plant hormone, and transport it to untouched cells. The untouched cells on the outside of a bend grow faster than the touched or contact cells. This causes the tendril or vine to curve toward the side of contact. It's almost a miracle how that happens!

When I was a boy, my brothers and I had to go through certain areas of the cornfields on our Seneca, Wisconsin farm and pull away the morning glories that wrapped around a corn stalk. We didn't know at the time that we were at war with thigmotropism.

Another tropism is *phototropism*, with light as the stimulus. Some sunflowers exhibit this phenomenon when young. The sunflower plant head bends toward a light source, the sun, allowing more light to reach more cells to produce photosynthesis. That same plant growth hormone, auxin, moves to the dark side of the stem. The dark side grows longer, causing the plant head to bend toward the light.

Q24: How do some plants eat flies?

There are about 474 kinds of carnivorous, or meat-eating, plants, but the best known is the Venus flytrap. These plants move very fast to catch a bug. If an insect touches the trigger hairs on the leaf, the leaf folds up suddenly and traps the bug inside. The plant secretes, or gives off, fluids (enzymes) that digest the insect. The Venus flytrap is aptly classified as a "snap trap" plant.

Plants that get a portion of their meal from animals, typically insects, tend to thrive in soils that are thin and low in nitrogen. Nitrogen is what the Venus flytrap is after. Bogs and rock outcroppings are places where the Venus flytrap can be found.

Some plants will capture their dinner with sticky fluids, and others will attract bugs and drown them in nectar and rainwater. There are a few underwater meat-eating plants that take in tiny water insects. The marsh pitcher plants trap their quarry in a rolled leaf. The leaf has a sac of digestive enzymes.

The butterwort and sundew plants have a "flypaper trap," a sticky glue on their leaves. Small flying insects are captured and devoured. The bladderwort plant develops a partial vacuum inside a bladder sealed with a hinged door.

As a rule, plants that eat meat (carnivores) live where other plants fail. They can survive in places where there is abundant light but poor soil conditions. Many struggle in our North Country, because the supply of insects is just not there. Others do not eat insects in the winter, switching to another diet or shutting down growth.

Q25: Why do chickens and turkeys have dark meat and white meat?

The color of meat depends on the concentration of a protein called myoglobin. This myoglobin protein delivers oxygen to muscles—oxygen they need for sustained work and stress. Birds that fly long distances to migrate or find food need the endurance that myoglobin provides. Wild birds we eat, such as quail, duck, pigeon, and geese, all have dark meat.

Chickens and turkeys don't fly any great distance. They are walkers. Their leg muscles need a lot of myoglobin protein, hence the dark drumstick meat. Turkey or chicken breasts have white muscle meat because those muscles don't need much myoglobin.

The domestic chicken or turkey lives a serene life with food provided. The only time they fly is for roosting or nesting, and then for only short times and distances. Their breast meat is white because their chest muscles get energy from glycogen, not myoglobin. Chickens and turkeys are about the only birds that have white meat on the breasts and wings.

The scientific community refers to the active dark meat muscles as slow-twitch fibers. Slow-twitch fibers are built for endurance. Turkeys and chickens, with slow-twitch fibers in their legs and thighs, can run around all day without getting tired.

Fast-twitch muscles are designed for bursts of energy, but they tire quickly. Their fuel is glycogen, a carbohydrate stored in tissue. The breast muscles of chickens and turkeys don't work hard for long, hence the white meat.

Which is better for you? That debate arises at Thanksgiving dinners and other festive occasions. Dark meat is rich in nutrients and vitamins B6, B12, niacin (vitamin B3), folate (a B vitamin), and minerals such as zinc, selenium, and phosphorus. So dark meat is considered to have more nutrition, but the difference is not huge.

Niacin helps build and maintain healthy skin, and aids in digestion and absorption of food. Vitamin B6 is necessary for protein metabolism. Zinc, a trace mineral, is used for growth and reproduction. Zinc also supports immunity, wound healing, and the sense of taste and smell.

White meat, however, is leaner and lower in fat. White meat may be favored by people who read the bathroom scales. These folks might go for a 4.6-ounce (130-gram) skinless chicken breast that has 192 calories and less than 3 grams of fat.

The difference is not that great. A turkey or chicken drumstick (dark meat) may be favored by kids, who like to pick up their food.

Human muscle, by the way, is also made of a combination of white and dark meat. Pigs, cows, sheep, and most mammals are built the same way.

(With thanks to Joan Kortbein, RD.)

Chapter Three

The Science of
Food and Drink

Q26: *What are powdered eggs made of?*
. . . .

Powdered eggs, which have the water removed from them, have some advantages over fresh eggs. They cost less. Their weight is reduced. They require less storage space. Their shelf life can be extended from 5 to 10 years. There is no need to refrigerate them. Powdered eggs are ideal for camping trips, troops in the field, and navies at sea. A bonus of powdered eggs is eliminating the possibility of bacterial contamination, such as salmonella.

The technique for making powdered eggs was developed in England by Albert Grant in the 1930s. He was a cake manufacturer importing eggs from China. The company realized that 90 percent of an egg was water, so it set up a freeze-drying plant in Singapore to perfect the dried-egg technique.

When World War II started, Grant transferred his operation to Argentina. The British government copied the process without paying Grant, and powdered eggs became a staple in the British and US militaries.

Powdered eggs are made commercially in a spray dryer. The liquid egg is beat into slurry and sprayed from a nozzle into a blast of hot air. The water content is removed. Powdered milk and many pharmaceuticals are made in the same fashion.

Powdered eggs can be made in home dehydrators, such as Snackmaster and Ronco. Obtainable from big-box stores, these dehydrators operate by slightly heating the food to release the moisture. Fans remove the moisture-laden air and draw in drier air. It can take hours or several days to sufficiently reduce the moisture content of some foods.

Eggs have come under fire at various times as being high in cholesterol, but eggs are very nutritious and a foundational item in baking. They are a low-cost, high-quality source of protein.

Q27: Why does soda pop explode when you shake the can?

When a can of soda is first opened, you hear a little hiss. That is the sound of carbon dioxide gas escaping from the can. The carbon dioxide gas is under pressure. Some gas has collected at the top of the can, and when the can is opened, it discharges with that familiar small hiss.

However, in the bottling process, most of the carbon dioxide has been dissolved in the liquid and held in a liquid state by the gas pressure above it. The carbon dioxide gives soda its fizzy quality.

If you shake the soda, something else goes on in the can. The carbon dioxide gas that was sitting on top of the liquid gets mixed around with the liquid soda below it. When you stop shaking the can, some of the gas returns to the top of the can. But many small bubbles of gas are stuck to the sides of the can.

When you open the can, the gas doesn't escape all by itself. The bubbles come rushing out from all parts of the inside of the can and bring liquid soda with them. Soda, gas, and bubbles spray over everything and create a delightful mess. In addition, the carbon dioxide gas that was dissolved in the soda no longer has high pressure on it, and the carbon dioxide is released from the soda.

Also, when the can is opened, the pressure in the can decreases, and volume of each bubble of gas stuck to the side increases. This is an excellent example of Boyle's Law, the relationship between pressure and volume of a confined gas.

There is a way to prevent this explosive mess from happening. Let's say a friend hands you a can of soda and you suspect that it has been shaken. You tap all around the sides of the container. About five or six thumb snaps ought to do it. This will dislodge the bubbles of carbon dioxide gas that have collected on the sides of the can. This works very well with regular sodas, but not so well with the diet ones because they contain much more carbon dioxide.

Tapping the top of the soda can does nothing because it is the sides and bottom that have the bubbles sticking to them.

A neat experiment and demonstration: Drop Mentos into diet soda, and the soda will foam violently. The roughness of the candy surface presents many little cavities and crannies that allow bubbles to form quickly. The process is called nucleation. In addition, the gelatin and gum arabic from the dissolving candy disrupt the surface tension of the liquid, and it takes much less work for the bubbles to expand.

Q28: Is Jell-O really made from horse hoofs?

Well, that's what we thought on the farm. If one of our three horses, Dolly, Prince, or Lightning, was not moving fast enough, that equine would receive the warning, "We'll send you to the Jell-O factory" or, "You're off to the glue factory." The horse paid no attention!

Jell-O is a registered trademark of Kraft Foods. Jell-O is about 87 percent sugar and 10 percent gelatin, with a tad of flavoring and coloring. The gelatin, the stuff that causes the wiggling, actually does come from pigskins, cattle bones, and cattle hides. Not to worry—it has all been cleaned up.

The skin, connective tissue, and bones of animals have a fibrous protein named collagen. When the collagen is treated with hot acid (type A) or alkali (type B), collagen turns into gelatin. The collagen is extracted into hot water, boiled down, and purified. It is colorless, translucent, and brittle when dry.

It melts into a liquid when warmed and turns into a solid when cooled. There is no collagen in hoofs.

Gelatin is widely used in foodstuffs, theater lightning equipment, capsules for medicines, glues, photo paper, soft drinks, sandpaper, match heads, cosmetics, playing cards, and glossy papers. Foods that contain lots of gelatin include marshmallows, candies, gummy bears, jams, yogurt, cream cheese, and margarine.

Ammunition manufacturers and gun makers shoot into blocks of gelatin. Ballistic gelatin closely simulates muscle tissue. The shells of paintballs are made of gelatin, the same stuff that drug capsules use. Ever see those translucent windowpanes in gingerbread houses? They're made of gelatin. Serious swimmers use gelatin in their hair. The colder pool water will not dissolve the gelatin. Some athletes claim that gelatin relieves knee joint pain and stiffness.

Jell-O was invented by Pearl B. Wait in Leroy, New York. Around 1900, immigrants landing at Ellis Island in New York City were served Jell-O as a "Welcome to America" treat. Utah has named Lime Green Jell-O as their official state dessert. Cranberry Jell-O seems to be very popular in November and December.

Q29: Does drinking milk make kids grow taller?

Studies from the American Society for Nutrition show that young children who have a long history of not drinking milk tend to have "less stature and high adiposity." Put simply, they tend to be short and fat.

The amount, the society admits, is very slight. Genetics plays a greater role than milk-drinking habits do in determining how tall a person will be in adulthood.

"The milk from breastfeeding is necessary for infant growth across all mammalian species, and humans are the only species of mammals that not only raises their young using the milk of another animal, but also consumes this milk in later life," says Dr. Robert Ashley from UCLA Health.

But what is the effect of drinking milk beyond the time of breastfeeding? The latest large study, completed in 2017 in Canada, found that children who drank 3 cups (0.7 liter) of cow milk a day were 0.6 inch (1.5 centimeters) taller than those who drank the same amount of non-cow milk daily. Non-cow milk means they could be drinking soy, almond, or goat milk.

Kids who drank 3 cups (0.7 liter) per day of soy, almond, or goat milk were 0.6 inch (1.5 centimeters) shorter than kids who did not drink any of those non-cow milks. What a kick in the head: Drinking soy, almond, or goat milk makes a kid shorter than if he or she did not drink that stuff. The study threw in goat milk in the same category as soy and almond milk.

The Canadian study, and Dr. Ashley's interpretation, give possible explanations. Size, including height, is linked to the intake of proteins. Cow's milk contains proteins in the casein and in the whey. Cow's milk also contains insulin-like growth factor 1 (IGF-1), which promotes bone and cartilage formation and hence greater height.

Two ideas came out of the study. One is that plant-based milks, soy and almond, do not contain as much protein and fat as cow milk. The other is that goat milk is not equivalent to cow milk. Children who don't drink cow milk may not get the calories and protein (or growth factor) needed for maximum growth.

There is another twist to this narrative. Kids with food allergies are less likely to drink cow milk. Food allergies have been associated with decreased height and weight. So, the allergies may be a factor in the link between milk and height.

Milk is high in calcium, which plays an important role in bone health, contributing to bone mass and density, and high in mineral content. In youth, a diet rich in calcium and protein can fortify the tender bone structure, preventing injury or harm that can stunt natural growth. Similarly, high bone mass and density could prevent osteoporosis in later life.

Any mention of milk brings me back to my days on the farm outside of Seneca, Wisconsin, in Crawford County, milking four cows by hand both morning and night. Oh, the neighbors had milking machines, but not the Scheckel family. I have memories of squirting the barn cats and milk fights with my two brothers, complete with matted hair. We drank whole milk, churned our own butter, and made our own ice cream. We had a milk separator, selling the cream to the cheese factory in Seneca. The skim milk was mixed with ground oats to make slop for the hogs.

Q30: *What is vitamin D?*

Vitamin D is a nutrient that supports the absorption of calcium and phosphorus. Vitamin D is good for bone, teeth, muscles, heart, prostate, colon, breast, and a positive mood. More than 500 studies back up the role of vitamin D in boosting the immune system.

Vitamin D stimulates the absorption of calcium for strong bones and teeth. A lack of vitamin D causes rickets in children. Rickets is the defective mineralization of bones, leading to weak and soft bones. In adults, a deficiency of vitamin D causes osteomalacia, a softening of the bones. That means muscle weakness, bone pain, and bone fractures.

Our body gets the vitamin D it needs from two different sources: from the foods we eat, especially eggs, butter, fish (halibut, salmon, tuna), and cod liver oil, and by absorbing sunlight through the skin. Vitamin D is manufactured by humans when the skin is exposed to sunlight. For us folks living in the northern climes, getting enough sunlight in the winter time can be a problem. We don't get sufficient UV (ultraviolet) rays from the sun in that long spell from November to March. It is little wonder that vitamin D is called the "sunshine vitamin."

When the skin absorbs sunshine, the ultraviolet rays stimulate or activate a form of cholesterol in the skin and convert it to vitamin D. That conversion, which begins in the skin, continues through the liver and kidneys and stimulates bones to absorb calcium.

Not everyone gets the same amount of vitamin D. It depends on your location on planet Earth, your skin color, and the time of the year. Non-white skin requires more sunlight. The further north you live, the fewer UV rays you get. If you live in northern Europe or the northern part of the United States, you might need a vitamin D supplement, especially during the winter months.

Calcium absorption is the only body process that requires vitamin D. However, it is widely believed that vitamin D has many anticancer properties, particularly against breast and colon cancer. Lack of vitamin D has been associated with multiple sclerosis, high blood pressure, and congestive heart disease.

Rickets was common among malnourished children of the Victorian era. Lately, there has been a slight rise in the number of cases. In the United States, cases typically are reported to occur in breastfed infants of African American mothers, most often those who are vegetarian.

Certain Middle Eastern countries have also seen a recent rise due to religious customs that require women to veil themselves. This reduces sun exposure and predisposes mothers and their breastfed infants to vitamin D deficiency.

We can also point to our modern lifestyle. Anyone who works indoors, lives indoors, wears long-sleeved clothing, and never gets out in the sun is put at higher risk.

People with an inflammatory bowel disease, such as Crohn's disease, are at risk. There has been some recent research that indicates that vitamin D provides protection from hypertension, cancers, and autoimmune diseases.

There are two ways to determine if a person is low on vitamin D. The doctor can test for vitamin D as part of a medical exam. The alternative is a purchased home test kit available from a drugstore. The user puts a few drops of blood on a strip, sends it in to the lab, and the results come back in a few weeks. The "normal" level is about 30 nanograms per milliliter (ng/ml).

The common recommendation for adults is 1,000 International Units (IU) per day of vitamin D_3. It is available over the counter at pharmacies and department stores.

Q31: Why doesn't regular corn pop like popcorn?

Not all corns are created equal. Of the five different types of corn—dent, flint, pod, sweet, and popcorn—only popcorn will pop consistently. Popcorn kernels contain water, ideally a bit more than 13 percent. The water is stored in a small circle of soft starch. Surrounding the soft starch is a very hard enamel-like starch. When the popcorn kernel is heated, the water inside heats up and starts to expand. The job of the hard starch is to resist the expanding water for as long as possible.

After some time, the water expands with such pressure that the hard starch gives way and the water bursts out, causing the popcorn kernel to explode. That soft starch pops free, and the kernel turns inside out. The water, converted into steam, is released and the corn kernel is popped.

Those other four varieties of corn can efficiently store water.

But their outer starch is not hard enough to withstand the water pressure of the expanding kernel, so nothing pops.

Popcorn is a member of the grass family, and scientifically known as *Zea mays everta*, a type of maize. It is a whole grain. There are other grains that will "pop," among them sorghum, quinoa, millet, and amaranth. All these grains have a hard moisture-sealed hull and a dense starchy interior. Sorghum is popular in the South.

We have all experienced leftover unpopped kernels, referred to in the industry as "old maids." These kernels did not pop because there was not enough moisture to create enough steam for an explosion.

We grew our own popcorn on the Scheckel farm outside of Seneca, TK. We cultivated both "white" and "yellow" popcorn. The yellow popcorn flakes were larger than the white. We found that popcorn popped best when it was stored in the cool dry basement for several months to about a year. It was probably that moisture thing. We made our own popcorn balls with a gooey sugar mixture. We also threaded popcorn on a string and wound the popcorn string around the Christmas tree.

Popcorn is quite nutritious, high in dietary fiber and antioxidants, free of sugar and salt, and low in calories and fat. Popcorn is very good for a person, if not slathered with salt and butter or oleo. Movie popcorn is loaded with . . . let's just say, a lot of stuff. Cracker Jack is caramel-covered popcorn with peanuts added.

Are puffed wheat and puffed rice the same as popcorn? They're similar. Those puffed grains are made by putting whole grains under high pressure with steam in a containment vessel. The vessel's pressure is suddenly released, and the steam that was entrapped in the soft material (endosperm) of the kernel will flash and bloat, increasing the kernel's volume to many times its original size.

Additional facts: Six different towns in the United States bill themselves as "Popcorn Capital of the World." All are in the Midwest. January 19 is National Popcorn Day in the United States. Orville Redenbacher made quite a name for himself in the popcorn business. Born on a farm in Brazil, Indiana, in 1907, Redenbacher played in the high school band, graduated from Purdue University where he was a track star, was a county agriculture agent, outlived two wives, and had captured a third of the popcorn business by 1970. On September 4, 2012, Valparaiso, Indiana, unveiled a statue of Redenbacher at the city's annual popcorn festival.

Q32: Why is water blue in the ocean but clear in a cup?

Pure water doesn't absorb or reflect much light. The light passes right through it. Water will absorb infrared and ultraviolet light, but not visible light. The color of water is determined by the selective absorption and reflection of white light. If tiny particles are suspended in the water, they may reflect light in a process known as scattering. The tiny particles act as little mirrors.

The short answer is that nothing in the water in your glass reflects light. Nothing in the water bounces or bends light. It's the same reason that air is clear and glass is clear. If glass is perfectly clear and smooth, with no wrinkles so that light is not distorted, then people have been known to walk right into it. Birds fly into glass windowpanes quite often.

However, it turns out that even pure water scatters blue light to some extent. When water is deep enough, you begin to see that blue color reflecting back at you. This is why water in a swimming pool appears bluish even though there is no light from the sky hitting it. The deep end probably looks bluer than the shallow end of the pool. Chemicals added to the water also affect the color you see.

Large bodies of water, such as rivers, lakes, and oceans can appear quite blue. Some of the blue comes about because the surface of the water reflects the blue light of the sky. The other factor is the scattering of blue light mentioned above. The scientific name is Rayleigh scattering.

Almost all water has some small particles in it. Scattering from suspended particles gives rise to various colors. High amounts of dissolved lime give Havasu Falls in Arizona a turquoise color. The Red Sea has occasional blooms of red algae. Some mountain lakes and streams have finely ground rock, or glacial flour, producing a lake of beautiful turquoise. The particles are so fine that they stay suspended in the water and do not settle out.

Color showing up in drinking water can be a warning that you shouldn't drink it. A green tint could mean copper leaching into the water. Red might indicate rust in the steel pipes. Black could come from the bacteria in a hot water tank whose thermostat has been turned down to about 120°F (48.8°C) instead of the factory-set 145°F (62.8°C). Tannins are organic matter from areas that are high in decaying vegetation, usually pumped from shallow wells found in swampy or coastal areas. The water may take on a yellowish hue but does not pose a health hazard.

Ice is interesting. If water freezes without any air in it, the ice is crystal clear. If any air bubbles or impurities are trapped inside, the ice is cloudy or whitish looking. Snow, which is full of air-ice boundaries, looks completely white.

Where does the white go when snow melts? Snowflakes have a six-sided or hexagonal symmetry. When light hits a snowflake, some light is reflected to our eye, and some penetrates the snow crystal, where it is bent or refracted. Because a snowflake has an intricate and complex structure, light hits many internal crystal faces and bounces around inside the crystal. That combination of reflection and refraction is very efficient, and eventually almost all the light bounces back toward the light source and the observer. Since all the light going in is white and made up of the seven colors, all the light coming back out looks white.

When the snow melts, all those faces and facets are gone, and no light can bounce around and come back out of the snow crystals. The "white" has disappeared. We are left with clear water.

Q33: *Why are chili peppers hot?*

Chili peppers are hot because they contain a powerful and stable alkaloid called capsaicin. It's a crystalline substance that grows at the junction of the pepper's rib and pod walls. Chili peppers are the only peppers that contain capsaicin.

The chemistry of capsaicin dates back to 1846 when L. T. Thresh used organic solvents to remove capsaicin from pepper pods. Wilbur Scoville developed a scale in 1912 to rate the sting of peppers, sort of a "rule of tongue." Habanero peppers have the highest rating. Jalapeno peppers are really quite low on the Scoville heat scale. There is a newer scheme called the "Gillett Method" that uses liquid chromatography. This high-tech method directly measures the amount of capsaicin in a sample..

Capsaicin molecules bind directly to receptors on cells in your tongue. These receptors are found on cells that detect heat and cells that send messages of pain. The cells alert your brain that your tongue has run into something hot and painful, even though the pepper may be cool and is not doing your tongue any harm.

Many species in the plant kingdom produce fruit that animals like to eat. The seeds pass through the digestive tract and are dispersed, ensuring the survival of the species. Pepper plants use capsaicin as a defense mechanism, allowing them to choose the best transport animals. The burning taste prevents mammals from gnawing on the plant. However, birds are not affected by the sharp taste. Birds eat peppers, and their droppings disperse them. The seeds are ready to germinate. If mammals ate the peppers, their chewing might tear up the seeds, and they wouldn't germinate.

Capsaicin is used in some arthritis medications. It stimulates circulation and also helps release endorphins that relieve pain. Peppers are a great source of vitamins A, C, and E, and are rich in folic acids and potassium.

Capsaicin is the stinging ingredient in pepper spray used by police officers to subdue rioters. The same compound is put in repellent sprays to keep rogue animals out of gardens. Scientists have even developed a coating for the hulls of ships using capsaicin. It prevents barnacles from growing on the bottoms of ships.

Chapter Four

Remarkable People in Science

Q34: *How and why does a person become a scientist?*
. . . .

A person becomes a scientist by being curious about everything. These are people who want to know how things work and to understand the underlying principles of nature. Scientists and engineers are fascinated with the possible applications of their particular discipline. They want to make a difference in the world. They want to strive to find solutions to problems and to give people a better standard of living.

The word *scientist* can be interpreted several ways. We all use science in everyday life, some more than others. Many people work in the sciences as engineers, computer programmers, science journalists, technicians, medical professionals, chemists, physicists, geologists, statisticians, technicians, and analysts, to name a few. One could say that they are all scientists.

Our typical mental image of a scientist is a person, usually male, wearing a white flowing coat and working alone in a lab. There may be some of those, but they would be a minority. Scientists today are both male and female and work in settings ranging from backwater swamps to NASA research facilities. Few scientists work in isolation; most are part of a team of researchers.

There are many reasons people go into a science field. Many find gratification when exceeding their prior understanding or performance. They rejoice in going beyond the boundaries of what was previously understood. Many are interested in the career aspects of being a scientist, and some just sort of tumble into being a scientist by life circumstances.

The mass media does not always give a favorable view of scientists and what they do. There are "mad scientists" like Dr. Strangelove, just waiting to blow up the world. *Blade Runner, Alien, Back to the Future, The Rocky Horror Picture Show, The Human Centipede*, and *From Beyond* are just a few of the movies that give scientists a bad name.

The Big Bang Theory sitcom shows several socially inept nerds. The galling thing about this so-called comedy is the writer's frequent use of scientific references, terms, and technobabble that tends to give the program some semblance of respectability.

Barbara McClintock (1902–1992) was an American scientist and geneticist. She won the Nobel Prize in 1983 in Physiology or Medicine. Here is her take on being a scientist: "I was just so interested in what I was doing I could hardly wait to get up in the morning and get at it. One of my friends, a geneticist, said I was a child, because only children can't wait to get up in the morning to get at what they want to do."

That sense of satisfaction can be exemplified by President Dwight D. Eisenhower. No, Ike was not a scientist; he was a famous World War II general who served eight years as president of the United States. In 1968, a year before his death, Eisenhower was asked what he considered his most cherished accomplishment. Eisenhower replied, "I bought a run-down farm in Pennsylvania, improved it, and made it productive." It's that same thread of thinking that a scientist has. Leave the world a better place.

Most scientists, as a rule, believe that science is critical to our future. They take great satisfaction in solving problems. Modern medicine, transportation, communication, food production, our personal comfort of heating and cooling, have all been the result of the work of scientists. The Internet has been a marvelous tool to keep people connected.

Usefulness is not the whole story. Henri Poincaré (1854–1912), French mathematician, physicist, and engineer said, "The scientist does not study nature because it is useful; he studies it because he delights in it, and he delights in it because it is beautiful. If nature were not beautiful, it would not be worth knowing, and if nature were not worth knowing, life would not be worth living."

The Wall Street Journal recently published a poll ranking the best and worst jobs in the United States, according to the following five criteria: physical demands, work environment, income, stress, and hiring outlook. The top 30 jobs were all science-related.

So which people go into science? People who are curious, who find the world fascinating, who yearn to know how things work, who want to improve the lot of mankind, make our world a better place to live, who have hope for the future, who believe that the road ahead is brighter than the road behind, who relish the thrill of discovery, and who want to make a good living for themselves and their family.

Q35: *Who invented paper?*

On anybody's list of the top 10 inventions, you will find paper and its attendant printing press. Yes, you will also find the steam engine, the clock, antibiotics, tools, the automobile, the lightbulb, the laser, atomic energy, and a host of others. But it seems like paper makes it onto every list.

The first material close to paper dates to around 3500 BCE. The Egyptians used strips from papyrus reed, which they moistened, made into a crisscross pattern, and then pressed into sheets. Our word for paper comes from papyrus.

The inventor of paper like that we use today was a Chinese court official, Cai Lun. He started with bark from a mulberry tree, along with rags and bamboo fibers. He mixed them in water, pounded the mass, and poured the mixture onto a flat piece of woven cloth. When the water drained, the fibers were left on the cloth. They dried into a single sheet. Cai Lun presented his new material to the Emperor He of Han as a substitute for silk, which was too valuable to write on. The year was CE 105. Modern papermaking is modeled on the Cai Lun method.

When Johannes Gutenberg invented the printing press in about CE 1450, the demand for paper soared. From that moment on most anybody with a little money could become literate, educated, own books, and build up a library.

These days paper is made from fast-growing trees such as fir and pine. The wood is pulverized, mixed with water, heated, cleaned, whitened, and pressed into sheets.

The state of Wisconsin has a proud and storied paper-making history. A plentiful supply of fresh water is necessary, and the Fox and Wisconsin Rivers cut right through the state. The forests of northern Wisconsin provided the raw material. There were plenty of high-paying union jobs in the paper industry. But the industry also caused a huge amount of pollution, both in the air and the water. The Clean Water Act of 1972 went a long way to making both rivers cleaner. Salmon have returned to the Fox River. Numerous Clean Air Acts have had a similar effect on the air.

Some say that electronic media have lessened the need for paper used in books, newspapers, and magazines. Perhaps that is true to some extent. But *USA Today* has a circulation of 15 million. The Barnes and Noble stores sell a ton of books. There is nothing quite like the feel of a newspaper or book. Even electronic readers like Kindle and Nook do not quite have the feel of paper.

Q36: How did astronauts get to the moon?

Think about all the things you need when you go on a trip. You need a vehicle to travel in, and you need food, water, air to breathe, and someplace to go to the bathroom. The astronauts who traveled to the moon had a spacecraft named

Apollo that could hold three people and enough water and food to last a little more than a week. Their spacecraft home could keep them at just the right temperature. The food was in tubes and some was freeze-dried. The water was recycled through fuel cells.

They needed a rocket that could get them going fast enough so that it wouldn't take too much time. The Saturn V rocket got them going 25,000 miles (40,000 kilometers) per hour. That is equivalent to 7 miles (11 kilometers) per second.

Their Apollo command module spacecraft was launched on a path that would intersect the moon three days later. The three-man crew was put into a parking orbit around the moon. Two astronauts climbed into a lander, called the lunar module (LM). This LM left the command module and carried the two astronauts to the surface of the moon. One astronaut remained in lunar orbit in the command module.

On each trip, the astronauts stayed on the moon for up to three days doing science experiments and lunar exploration. The top part of the LM then became the ascent pod that blasted off from the moon, leaving its lower part on the moon. Luckily, leaving the moon didn't require a huge rocket, because the moon's gravity is so much weaker than the earth's.

The two astronauts joined up with the third astronaut in lunar orbit. They transferred their rock and soil samples, as well as film cartridges, to the command module.

They fired up the big rocket engine on the service module to change to an Earth return course. Three days later, the astronauts splashed down in the ocean.

In short, they had to go in stages, leaving behind parts of the rocket that had been used up. They needed the help of thousands of people on Earth who did not go with them. Just as we often need the help of friends and classmates to get things done, the astronauts needed people to build and launch their spacecraft, and to provide guidance to the moon and back.

The first landing on the moon was July 20, 1969. The last landing was in December 1972. Six successful moon landings and explorations were accomplished. Twelve astronauts have walked on the moon. The total cost of the Apollo program was around $20 billion.

The movie *Apollo 13*, featuring Tom Hanks as Commander James Lovell, is historically accurate and well done. After the initial 1969 landing, Apollo 13 was the one mission that was not successful in landing astronauts on the moon.

Q37: Did Archimedes really run naked through the streets of Syracuse shouting "Eureka?"

W ell, that's what history tells us. Archimedes, born in 281 BCE, was a Greek mathematician, inventor, and astronomer. As the legend goes, Hieron II, the king of Syracuse, had commissioned a goldsmith to make a crown for him from pure gold. When the crown was delivered, the king had some doubts about the goldsmith's honesty. The goldsmith could have easily mixed a less valuable metal, such as silver or copper, in place of the gold and kept some of the gold for himself.

Craftsmen knew how to mix gold with silver and copper. These alloys retain the rich color of gold even when significant amounts of other metals are added. But because these less valuable metals are a bit less dense than gold is, the goldsmith would have had to add a bit more metal than he stole, to keep the weight the same.

King Hieron II called in his buddy Archimedes and presented him with the job of finding out whether the crown was indeed pure gold or altered with some base material. Archimedes had to do what today is called nondestructive testing. He couldn't melt down the crown into a regularly shaped body in order to determine its density. He might be destroying a perfectly good crown.

The story goes that when Archimedes stepped into the bathtub, he realized that the volume of the overflow water was exactly equal to the volume of the part of his body that he placed in the water.

Archimedes saw a way to calculate the volume of any irregularly shaped solid object. If he put the crown into a container filled with water, he could measure the volume of the water that overflowed. The overflow volume would be equal to the volume of the crown.

So now Archimedes had the volume of the crown and its mass or weight. By dividing the mass by the volume, he could calculate the density. The density would be lower than that of pure gold if the crown were mixed with silver or copper.

What Archimedes found was that the volume was considerably greater than it should have been for a crown made of pure gold. The dishonest goldsmith was executed. The accidental and fortuitous discovery for Archimedes was not so good for the goldsmith.

Archimedes' principle states that a body immersed in a fluid experiences a buoyant force equal to the weight of the fluid it displaces. It would have been possible to compare the density of pure gold to the density of the crown by putting the crown on one side of a balance scale and an equal mass of gold on the other side of the balance arm. Then both samples could be immersed in water. When put in water, a fake crown, having more volume, would displace more water.

We can attribute a number of other inventions to Archimedes. He invented a screw-like device to lift or pump water. He developed numerous war machines, including the claw, a crane-like arm with a grappling hook that when suspended and dropped in the water could lift a ship, possibly sinking it. Archimedes also explained the principle of the lever and constructed an odometer to measure how far a cart traveled. He made devices to show the motion of the sun, moon, and five known planets, and offered many contributions to mathematics.

The famous mathematician met an unfortunate and untimely demise. Romans invaded his hometown of Syracuse in 212 BCE. Syracuse is a historic city in Sicily, the large Mediterranean island off Italy. Syracuse had a heavy Greek influence at the time.

During the Roman attack, Archimedes was drawing mathematical figures in the dirt with a stick. A Roman soldier commanded him to move on. Either Archimedes did not hear or he was too focused on his work to let a mere soldier distract him. Either way, the enraged legionnaire ran him through with his sword.

Was Archimedes really so excited about his solution to the gold crown problem that he failed to put his clothes on when he exited the bathtub and ran naked through the streets of Syracuse? Really not sure. Let's hope he brought a towel.

Q38: Who invented television?

Philo T. Farnsworth gets the credit for inventing the first all-electronic image pick-up device. That's a fancy way of saying he built the first video camera tube. He drew the concept on the blackboard for his science teacher when he was a sophomore at Rigby High School in Idaho in 1920.

There were already several dozen mechanical scanning devices, notably one built by Russian immigrant Vladimir Zworykin. But all those mechanical devices, with whirling moving parts, had severe limitations.

On September 7, 1927, Farnsworth's camera transmitted its first image, a straight line, to a receiver in another room. His backers in San Francisco wanted to know if they could make money from his invention. So the next image he sent was that of a dollar sign.

Farnsworth had to defend his television camera patent. His main antagonist was RCA's head, David Sarnoff. By 1935, the US Patent Office concluded that Farnsworth was the inventor, and RCA was forced to pay royalties on every TV they built. RCA engineers did go on to make many improvements in broadcast television.

Farnsworth's television camera was used to broadcast the 1936 Olympics to Germans in Berlin. Notables attending were Adolf Hitler, American runner Jesse Owens, and Louis Zamperini, Olympian and later World War II POW, subject of the book and 2014 film *Unbroken*.

Philo T. Farnsworth is a heroic figure in many respects. Born in a Utah log cabin in 1906, Farnsworth was the eldest of five children. As a teenager, he devoured technical magazines and dreamed of transmitting images electronically. While still in high school, he took classes at Brigham Young University. When his father died, he dropped out of school to support his younger siblings and eventually moved to California to carry out his experiments.

Farnsworth was a prolific inventor with 165 patents. He devised a nuclear device that became a ready source of neutrons. He developed a process to sterilize milk with radio waves, invented a fog-penetrating beam to guide ships and planes, and worked out a system of early warning signals for national defense.

Farnsworth invented submarine detection systems and developed an infrared telescope.

He enhanced radar with the circular sweep display that is the mainstay for modern air traffic control.

What a profound moment it must have been for the aging Farnsworth to watch Neil Armstrong and Buzz Aldrin climb down from the lunar module in July 1969, and to witness the two astronauts step onto the moon on live television. Decades earlier, he had invented the device that allowed him, along with 500 million people around the world, to see man walk on the moon.

Farnsworth married his college sweetheart, Elma Gardner. They had four boys. His life was not always easy. His company faltered in the late 1960s. He battled lifelong depression, sank into alcoholism in his final years, and died of pneumonia in 1971 at age 64. He is buried in Provo City, Utah.

A devout Mormon, Farnsworth did not take credit for his creative mind and vast scientific output. Shortly before his death, he wrote, "I know that God exists. I know that I have never invented anything. I have been a medium by which these things were given to the culture as fast as the culture could earn them. I give all the credit to God."

Q39: *Are some scientific discoveries made by accident?*

Yes, quite a few. Penicillin, X-rays, Teflon, the Rosetta Stone, vulcanized rubber, nylon, the laws of gravity, quinine, the electric battery, dynamite, the Dead Sea Scrolls, vaccinations, the big bang, radioactivity, saccharin, and Velcro are just a few.

A more accurate and better description would be to use the term *serendipity*. These were chance discoveries that led to momentous scientific developments. We should not discount the efforts and genius that went into these discoveries. Louis Pasteur said, "Chance favors the prepared mind." Careful observation, curiosity, a sense of timing and history, and just plain good luck are all involved.

Go ahead and pick one of the above. OK, it will be Teflon. On April 6, 1938, a young PhD graduate from Ohio State was a newly hired Du Pont chemist. Roy J. Plunkett and an assistant, Jack Rebok, were trying to develop a new nontoxic refrigerant.

Dr. Plunkett opened a tank of tetrafluoroethylene (TFE). No gas came out. The two young scientists could have thrown the tank out and pulled out a new one to continue their experiment. But they were curious. They knew the valve was not defective because they could run a wire into the opening.

They sawed the tank open and looked inside. Within, they found a waxy white powder clinging to the inside walls of the tank. They knew enough chemistry to realize that the gas (the one with the long name above) had combined with something to form a solid material, a new polymer, or long-chain molecule.

The waxy white powder had some neat properties. It was not affected by acids, bases, or heat, and no solvent could dissolve it. It had extremely low surface friction, i.e., it was slippery. They called it Teflon.

The scientists working on the first atomic bomb in the early 1940s needed a material for gaskets that would resist the very corrosive gas, uranium hexafluoride, used to extract the Uranium-235 needed to build the first atomic bomb. The DuPont company molded Teflon into valves and gaskets for this purpose. The public did not know anything about Teflon until after the war.

The first Teflon-coated muffin tins and frying pans came out in 1960. Results were not that good. It was difficult to get the Teflon to bond to metal surfaces, and too many people used scouring pads, which they had traditionally employed on their metal cookware. Off came the Teflon. DuPont finally hit the Teflon jackpot in 1986 with their new generation Silver Stone Supra, which was twice as durable.

We might know Teflon for cookware, but Teflon is also one of the few substances that the body doesn't reject. Teflon is used on heart pacemakers and sections of material used to take the place of the aorta. Teflon is used for artificial corneas, substitute bones in the chin and nose, hip and knee joints, ear parts, heart valves, sutures, dentures, and bile ducts.

Teflon is applied to the outer layers of space suits. Nose cones and space fuel tanks are coated with Teflon. Spacecraft that have traveled to the moon and beyond had wiring and cables insulated with Teflon. Teflon can resist the ultraviolet radiation of the sun.

In 1951, Roy Plunkett gave a talk to a scientific convention in Philadelphia detailing his accidental discovery. Attendees were given a Teflon-coated muffin pan to take home. Plunkett retired from DuPont in 1975, was inducted into the Inventors Hall of Fame in 1985, enjoyed fishing and golfing near his home in Corpus Christi, Texas, and died in 1994 at age 83. His greatest joy, he said, was getting calls and letters from people who were alive because of a Teflon pacemaker or aorta.

Q40: *What scientist's work has saved the most lives?*

There are men who are responsible for taking lives, and those who are known for saving lives. Hitler, Mussolini, Tojo, Stalin, and Pol Pot are guilty of killing and destroying millions of humans. They are well known, filling the pages of history books.

Some people who save lives also get a lot of ink in the history books. Edward Jenner, an English physician and scientist, pioneered the smallpox vaccine and is called the "father of immunology." Louis Pasteur, building on the work of Jenner, developed a food processing technique, pasteurization, which destroys bacteria by heating liquids and allowing them to cool. He was prominent in developing the germ theory of disease, and he gave us vaccinations for anthrax and rabies. Dr. Jonas Salk developed the polio vaccine. Mother Teresa, a Catholic nun, founded the Missionaries of Charity, which has 5,000 sisters active in 133 countries and runs soup kitchens, dispensaries, orphanages, schools, and hospices.

But Norman Borlaug has saved more lives than any other human being, as many as one billion people. A plant breeder and biologist, Borlaug was born in 1914 in Cresco, Iowa. Called "the Father of the Green Revolution," he spent his career fighting world hunger. He passed most of his life in the developing countries of Mexico, Pakistan, India, and regions of Africa.

In the mid-1960s, mass starvation was predicted in the developing world after two successive droughts in India. Biologist Paul Ehrlich wrote in his best-selling book, *The Population Bomb*, "The battle to feed all of humanity is over. In the 1970s and 1980s, hundreds of millions of people will starve to death in spite of any crash programs embarked upon now." Norman Borlaug was determined not to accept this verdict.

Working in Mexico, Borlaug and his team developed a breed of dwarf wheat that resisted a wide variety of pests and diseases. Borlaug-bred wheat had shorter, thicker stalks or stems that could support larger seed heads. The shorter wheat accepted fertilizer and did not have to compete as much for sunlight, so a farmer could have more plants per acre. Yields increased by two, three, and even four times. In 1963, the Mexican wheat harvest was six times larger than in 1944 when he arrived.

Borlaug's team also developed wheat varieties that were adapted to tropical climates. In the 1960s, he took his wheat varieties to Pakistan and India. Pakistan doubled its wheat production in just five years. By 1974, India was self-sufficient in the production of wheat. Borlaug went on to develop a wide variety of rice plants that produced outstanding yields. In 1970, he was awarded the Nobel Peace Prize in recognition of his work fighting world hunger.

There may be a lesson here. Paul Ehrlich was just one of many scientists who predicted mass starvation, even extinction, due to overpopulation. We see the same gloom-and-doom predictions from some scientists and politicians on climate change. Yes, global warming could turn out to be a huge problem, but that doesn't mean we should throw up our hands and give up. Instead, we need to use our determination and powers of invention to address the problem.

And you never know what can inspire a person to make contributions to mankind. At age 21, Norman Borlaug took a job as leader of a CCC (Civilian Conservation Corps) group. He needed a job to finance his college education. Many of the people working for him had been starving. "I saw how food changed them. All of this left scars on me."

Borlaug was not without his critics. Some environmentalists opposed genetic crossbreeding and heavy use of fertilizers as unnatural or harmful. Borlaug dismissed these environmental lobbyists. "They've never experienced the physical sensation of hunger. They do their lobbying from comfortable office suites in Washington or Brussels."

Borlaug met his future wife, Margaret Gibson, while waiting on tables at a coffee shop when in college. They were married for sixty-nine years and had three children, one of whom died shortly after birth due to spina bifida. Norman Borlaug died in 2009 of lymphoma in Dallas at age 95.

An estimated one billion lives saved. That's a quite a legacy.

Chapter Five

The Science of the Heavens and Earth

Q41: *Why does lightning come in different colors?*
. . . .

I ndeed, lightning takes on different colors depending on the weather conditions, clouds, moisture content of the air, and how far away the lightning flash occurs.

White lightning is an indication of very low humidity. White lightning is often spotted out West, especially in desert regions. Most forest fires are started by this type of lightning.

Yellow or orange lightning is observed when there is a lot of dust in the air. Yellow-orange lightning is also seen if the lightning is far on the horizon, for the same reason that the sun or moon appears reddish orange when it is on the horizon. The shorter wavelengths of blue and green are scattered by water vapor, pollutants, and dust in the air. All that is left to reach the eye are the longer waves of red, yellow, and orange.

The presence of hail in clouds will make lightning appear blue. A lot of rain in a thunderstorm will allow the lightning take on a reddish tint.

The color of the bolt is also influenced by how hot it is. The temperature of the air around a lightning bolt is about 50,000°F (28,000 °C). That's about five to six times hotter than the surface of the sun. The hotter the lightning, the closer it will be to a blue-white color. A cooler bolt will tend toward a reddish color. This is the same idea as heating a filament, a horseshoe, or any type of metal.

Lightning is a result of both incandescence and luminescence. Incandescence is due to the high temperature and luminescence is because of exciting or activating the nitrogen gas in the atmosphere. Incandescence is what goes on in a regular old-fashioned screw-in lightbulb. Luminescence is what takes place in a fluorescent lightbulb.

A neat exercise is to determine how far lightning is away from you. Light travels a million times faster than sound. For all practical purposes, the light from lightning takes no time at all to reach you. But it takes five seconds for sound to go one mile (1.6 kilometers).

Count the time between flash and thunder and divide that number by five to get the distance in miles. If you count to five, the lightning is 1 mile (1.6 kilometers) away. If you count to ten, the lightning is 2 miles (3.2 kilometers) away.

A lightning bolt is powerful. A single stroke is several hundred million volts and several hundred thousand amperes. If we could harness the power of lightning, we would never have any energy problems in the world.

People have been struck by lightning and survived. As long as the bolt doesn't go through the heart or spinal column, you're good to go with, at worst, severe burns and burst eardrums.

Roy Sullivan, a park ranger in Virginia's Shenandoah National Park, was struck by lightning seven times between 1942 and 1977. Strangely, he took his own life in 1983 at age 71.

Q42: *Why do glaciers move south?*
. . . .

Glaciers have been called rivers of ice, which is a pretty good description since glaciers move from a higher to a lower elevation. Glaciers can move in any direction: north, east, south, or west, depending on the lay of the land. In the northern hemisphere, more glaciers move, by chance, in a southern direction compared to any other direction. The only criterion for glacier movement is from a higher point to a lower point, which means moving down a valley.

There are two types of glaciers: Alpine glaciers form in the mountains and flow down the mountains by gravity; ice sheets cover huge expanses of land. There are only two ice sheets on Earth: Antarctica and Greenland.

Glaciers have an area of accumulation and an area of ablation. The accumulation area is where the temperature is cold; snow collects, adding mass to the glacier. Snow that builds up in the first winter is referred to as a neve. If the snow stays around for more than a year it is called a firn, and then the weight will compact the snow into glacial ice.

After years and years of compaction, air is forced out of the ice. The ice absorbs all the colors or wavelengths of light except blue. Blue is reflected to our eyes. That's why the ice takes on a bluish color.

The ablation area is where the temperature is warmer and parts of the glacier melt. Often, the ablation area is where the glacier meets the ocean. The glacier extends out onto the water where it floats. The tides flex the ice shelf up and down until huge chunks fall off the glacier. The best place to witness this calving is one of the bays in Alaska, such as Glacier Bay National Park or Prince William Sound. Cruise ships visit both these sites.

Most alpine glaciers rest on the slopes of mountains. The huge weight of the glacier causes a small amount of ice at the bottom to melt in a process termed regelation. This thin layer of water reduces friction enough that the glacier can slide down the mountain. Basal slip is the term used.

A good place to visit alpine glaciers is in Glacier National Park in Montana. Here the glaciers don't meet the sea. They simply melt. You can easily walk on the Columbia Ice Field in the Canadian Rockies near Jasper and Banff, Alberta. Buses take you right up onto the glacier. Athabasca Glacier is nearby. Helicopters land you on the glacier.

In Juneau, Alaska, the Mendenhall Glacier is right outside the city. The citizens have built a beautiful visitor center with excellent views of the Glacier and Mendenhall Lake. Footpaths lead right up to the edge of the glacier.

During the last ice age, about 10,000 years ago, about one third of Earth was covered by ice. Today, only about 10 percent of the landmass of planet Earth is covered with glaciers. Still, nearly 75 percent of the fresh water on Earth is locked in glaciers today. Glaciers can vary in thickness from 30 feet to several hundred feet. The Antarctic ice is more than 2 miles (3.2 kilometers) thick in places.

Most glaciers move only a few inches a year. The world's fastest-moving glacier is the Jakobshavn Glacier in Greenland. It moves about 2 miles (3.2 kilometers) per year.

Since the Industrial Revolution, humans been pouring a lot of carbon dioxide into the atmosphere. The global warming has caused many glaciers to retreat during our lifetime.

Q43: How are volcanoes formed, and how do they erupt?

Earth's surface consists of huge plates that fit together like a jigsaw puzzle. These plates float on a liquid-like layer called the mantle. These large tectonic plates are in very slow but constant motion. Sometimes the plates move toward each other and sometimes they move apart. Friction between moving plates causes earthquakes and volcanic eruptions near the edges of the plates.

Periodically, the edge of a tectonic plate will sink down under the edge of another plate into the mantle layer. In the mantle, the rocks come under tremendous pressure. They become very hot and melt into magma at about 5,000°F (2,760°C). This magma is always working its way upward toward the earth's surface. When magma reaches the earth's surface we call it lava. The lava emerges through cracks known as vents. When layer after layer of lava builds up and hardens, a volcano is formed.

There are various types of volcanoes, depending on what kinds of material make up the lava, the amount of gas trapped in the lava, and how much pressure builds up. When the molten rock moves to the surface through the earth's crust and releases the pent-up gases, volcanoes erupt.

Volcanoes occur most often at plate boundaries. The best known is the Ring of Fire, a horseshoe-shaped string stretching from the western side of South America, up along the western side of North America, across the Bering Sea, down to Japan, Philippines, and into Southeast Asia. This Ring of Fire contains about two thirds of active volcanoes today.

The most active volcano in the world is Kilauea on the Big Island of Hawaii. Kilauea, inside Volcanoes National Park, has been in constant eruption since 1983, but really started acting up in mid-June of 2018. Nearly 1,000 building have been destroyed, and more to go.

Kilauea is a great tourist attraction with a beautiful visitor center. During the current active eruption, most of Volcanoes National Park has been closed, but at other times adventurous souls can walk over the hot lava till their soles start to melt. They can also watch the lava fall into the Pacific Ocean, especially from the air or ocean. But don't get too close! In July 2018, a tourist boat off the coast moved too close to the volcano. A big chunk of hot lava ripped through the boat, injuring 23.

There are more than 1,500 active volcanoes on Earth. Mount Saint Helens, in southwest Washington State, erupted on Sunday, May 18, 1980, killing 57 people. Good portions of Washington and Oregon were covered with ash. *Esquire* magazine named Mount Saint Helens "ash hole of the year."

Mount Saint Helens has two do-not-miss attractions. The Forest Learning Center has an unforgettable "eruption chamber," life-like forests, beautiful views of the mountain, and many exhibits. The Johnson Ridge Observatory, open only during the summer months, shows a big-screen movie. When the movie finishes, the curtains open and the visitor enjoys a spectacular view of Mount Saint Helens.

David Johnson, a volcanologist, was camped out on this ridge when the volcano blew. His final words, heard through his radio, were, "Vancouver, Vancouver, this is it." His body has never been found. The Johnson Ridge Observatory is named in his honor.

The most destructive volcano in modern times erupted in 1985 in Colombia. Mud flows buried 23,000 people in just a few hours.

Venus is dotted with thousands of volcanoes and Io, a moon of Jupiter, has many active volcanoes. It is believed there was volcanic activity on the moon billions of years ago.

Q44: What is frac(ture) sand and what is fracking?

Fracture sands are used in extracting oil and gas by creating cracks in underground rock formations through the process known as fracking. Not all sands are created equal. The sand particles that oil companies want must be rounded like marbles and very strong and hard, almost pure quartz. One could think of these sands as tiny diamonds or miniature snowballs. The sand granules must be extremely hard so they won't crush or break down in an oil wellhead.

Our area of Wisconsin was very stable millions of years ago, with no volcanoes, mountains, or earthquakes. The sea flooded this vast low central continent and helped purify the sands. The sand grains ended up here 500 million years ago, even before the formation of the Great Lakes.

Frac sand is used to stimulate oil and gas wells. It is mixed with water and pumped at extremely high pressure into oil and natural gas wells. That high pressure causes the underground formation to crack or fracture, allowing the water and sand mixture to enter and extend the crack further into the formation.

The slurry of sand and water blasts apart the rock, and the strong round sand grains hold the fractures open so that oil and natural gas can make their way to the surface. Frac sand, also called a proppant, prevents the fractures from closing when the high-pressure injection is stopped.

Due to rising oil and gas prices, there has been a rush to go after oil and natural gas locked in shale deposits in Canada, especially at the Horn River Basin in northeast British Columbia. Some frac sands have been sent to Texas, Oklahoma, Wyoming, Colorado, and Canada.

The demand for frac sand has increased due to the type of gas drilling companies employ. They drill down and then drill horizontally. All those bore holes require frac sand.

Whenever any kind of mining takes place, there are concerns. People worry about the impact on land values, the amount and quality of groundwater, noise, pollution, and traffic. This is especially true for nearby home and land owners. The long-term effects of fracking are not well known.

Earthquakes have been linked to fracking. The quakes, some geologists report, are caused by fluid disposal in deep wells. The millions of gallons of waste fluids are usually pumped back into the earth via deep wastewater injection wells. The wastewater can lubricate or jack open fractures and faults, triggering earthquakes.

One of the unknowns is the dust created in the sand mining process. Very fine dust, from any number of sources, is not something a person wants in his or her lungs. We continue to hear about problems from rescue and clean-up workers around the World Trade Center site. That happened way back in 2001.

We've all seen mining operations. They're not always a pretty picture when operating. But we've seen areas in Kentucky and Tennessee that were strip-mined for coal, but have since been beautifully restored and reseeded, with new forests planted.

An argument could be made that we must go after these resources and reduce our dependence on imported foreign oil. Also, as a nation, we want to reduce emissions of carbon dioxide. Natural gas is cleaner than burning coal. Our coal-fired power plants spew huge amounts of carbon dioxide into the atmosphere.

Q45: *What causes the northern lights or aurora borealis?*

The scientific name for the northern lights is the aurora borealis. These shimmering lights have their origin in the sun. Solar activity causes a huge ejection of particles. The ions and atoms take two or three days to get to Earth, where they get caught in Earth's magnetic field. The flow of charged particles is termed the solar wind. These charged particles flow along the lines of the magnetic field in both polar regions of the earth. Collisions with oxygen and nitrogen atoms produce the dazzling light displays.

The vivid colors produced by the northern lights are very much akin to the colors formed in neon advertising signs we see in bars, barbershops, and stores. The physics is the same. Atoms are energized. Electrons going around the nucleus are made to go to orbits further away from the nucleus. When the electrons fall back to their normal orbit, the atom gives up its energy by emitting a little bit of visible light.

Collisions with oxygen yield green, the most common of all the aurora colors. Nitrogen gives red colors. The next most prominent colors are a mixture of light green and red, pure red, then yellow, which comes from a mixture of red and green light. Finally, and least common, there is pure blue.

The best time to observe the northern lights is from 9:00 p.m. to 1:00 a.m., and the best months are March, April, August, and September. The closer an observer is to the polar regions, the better the view. People living in Alaska and Greenland find the northern lights visible most nights of the year.

The earliest accounts of the aurora borealis date back to 567 BCE and appear on Babylonian clay tablets. The most spectacular display in modern times was on September 2, 1859, seen over the entire earth and recorded in ships' logs. The New York and Boston newspapers reported at the time that the northern lights were so brilliant that newspapers could be read at one o'clock in the morning.

The charged particles of the solar wind could do a lot of damage to us on Earth if not for the protection provided by our planet's atmosphere and magnetic field. Even with that protection, the northern lights can damage the electrical power grid on Earth and satellites in space.

The moon has neither an atmosphere nor a magnetic field. Astronauts working on the surface of the moon would be in grave danger when a big solar flare occurs. Astronauts in the International Space Station (ISS) are sometimes alerted to violent solar activity. In December 2006, a huge solar flare made the astronauts move to a more protected module inside the ISS.

Solar flares are brief eruptions of intense high-radiation energy from the sun. Associated with sunspots, they occur in an 11-year cycle of high and low magnetic activity. The most recent cycle of solar flares and sunspot activity peaked around 2014, and it is now reaching a low.

Predictions of solar flares are good for a few hours or one day at best. Predictions are based on satellite observations of sunspots and solar activity. The Geophysical Institute at the University of Alaska Fairbanks issues aurora forecasts. Magnetometers and particle detectors in satellites can tell if a "space weather storm" will be approaching in a few hours.

Q46: What is the warmest thing in our solar system?
. . . .

The highest temperature in our solar system is found in the core of the sun. The center of the sun is about 27 million°F (15 million°C). That's really, really, hot!

The surface of the sun is 10,000°F (5,500°C). The region above the surface, the corona, can get up to 4 million°F (2.2 million°C) due to the solar flares and coronal mass ejections.

Outside the sun, the core of Jupiter is about 50,000°F (28,000°C). The high temperature is due to the pressure of the mass of the planet pushing down and compressing the core.

The hottest surface of any planet would be found on Venus. The 800°F (430°C) temperature is due to dense carbon dioxide clouds and a runaway greenhouse effect. The clouds drip caustic sulfuric acid. Venus is hotter than Mercury, even though Mercury is closer to the sun. We will not be visiting either planet soon.

The core of the Earth is estimated to be about 9,800°F (5,400°C). The core consists of molten rock and iron. The movement of the molten interior is what gives our home Earth planet a magnetic field.

The hottest place on Earth is a desert in Iran. The Lut Desert is covered with dried black lava rock which that absorbs the heat of the sun. The 157°F (70°C) temperature does not allow bacteria to survive.

The hottest place in the United States is Death Valley. Late afternoon summertime temps can reach 130°F (54°C). My wife, Ann, and I visited Death Valley in August a few years ago. With a slight breeze, it feels like walking into a blowtorch! We headed to the Sierra Nevada Mountains the next day.

The temperature of the air around a lightning bolt is 50,000°F (28,000°C). That is hotter than the surface of the sun. The electrical discharge heats the air it passes through. The rapid expansion of heated air is termed thunder. A thermonuclear explosion, or hydrogen bomb, can generate temperatures of more than 100 million°F (56 million°C).

How do you convert from Celsius to Fahrenheit? Take the Celsius number, add 40, multiply by 1.8, and then subtract 40. As an example, let's take a body temperature of 37°C, add 40 to get 77, multiply by 1.8 to get 138.6, now subtract 40 to get 98.6°F.

When discussing high temperatures up in the thousands of degrees, simply take the Celsius and double it, and it is close enough: 10,000°C= 20,000°F.

By the way, Celsius is now the more accepted usage, not the term *centigrade*. Both are correct and understood by everyone worldwide. However, Celsius honors the inventor of the scale, Swedish astronomer, Anders Celsius (1701–1744.)

Q47: How does a black hole work?

A black hole is what is left over when a massive star has run out of fuel and collapsed. Why does that happen?

There are two main, competing processes that shape stars. The fusion reactions are like tiny hydrogen bombs going off and tend to make the star bigger. At the same time, gravity tends to crunch all solar material and make the star smaller. These two forces are balanced throughout a star's life, which typically lasts for billions of years.

The size of a star is determined by this balance between gravity, making it smaller, and explosive forces, making it bigger, and this balance shifts only at the end of a star's life, when the ultimate fate of any star is determined by its mass.

What happens to a star the size of our sun? When nearly all the hydrogen is converted to helium, gravity will dominate, and the sun will collapse, ignite the nuclear ashes of helium, and fuse them into carbon. The fusion of helium into carbon creates a tremendous amount of heat. The process creates energy that the star needs to resist the force of gravity that is trying to crush the star together. This also causes the star to light up.

The sun will expand to the size of the orbit of Mars, at which point it is a red giant. After a few million years, the helium in the sun's core will also run out, and the red giant will collapse. The outer layers will blow away in clouds of dust and gas, while the core itself cools into a white dwarf—and eventually, into a nearly invisible black dwarf. The entire process will take billions of years.

The story is quite different for a star three or four times the mass of the sun. Once nuclear fusion is done, the collapse doesn't stop. The star not only caves in on itself, but the atoms that make up the star collapse so there are no empty spaces within them. What is left is a core that is highly compressed, very massive, and very dense. Gravitation is so strong near this core that even light can't escape. The particles within the core have collapsed and crushed themselves out of visible existence. The star disappears from view and is now a black hole.

If we can't see black holes, how do we know they exist? Though they're not visible, we can detect or hypothesize about the presence of one by studying surrounding objects. Astronomers can see material swirling around or being pulled off a nearby visible star. The mass of a black hole can be estimated by observing the motion of nearby visible stars.

The core, or nucleus, of Galaxy NGC 4261, for example, is about the same size as our solar system, but it weighs 1.2 billion times as much as our sun. Such a huge mass for such a small disk indicates the presence of a black hole. The core of this galaxy contains a black hole with huge spiral disks feeding dust and material into it.

Q48: *Could we live on Mars?*

Yes, but it wouldn't be easy, and it would cost tons of money. It takes about eight months to get to Mars and eight months to get back. You would have to stay about two years on the surface of Mars before Earth and Mars are aligned properly for a return. You would need food and oxygen for a mission that would last more than three years.

Mars looks a lot like parts of Arizona, with rocks strewn among shifting sand dunes. The soil is reddish and the sky pinkish due to the iron oxide in the soil. The carbon dioxide atmosphere is extremely thin. It gets down to –220°F (–140°C) at night and up to 60°F (15.6°C) on summer days. Huge dust storms last for weeks. It's a hostile place.

Water was once plentiful on Mars and flowed in huge rivers. When the air thinned and air pressure decreased, the water evaporated. Today, some water is trapped in the soil and frozen in the permafrost.

The United States will continue to send unmanned vehicles to Mars. In about 10 to 15 years we'll send a robot to get soil and rock samples from Mars. The best guess is that it will be 50 to 100 years before we send people to Mars. Much depends on our economic conditions and our will to send a mission. Most likely, it would be a joint venture by several countries.

Speculation about traveling to and establishing a station on Mars was fueled by the book *The Martian* by Andy Weir, and the 2015 movie by the same name. Matt Damon plays astronaut Mark Watney, who is presumed dead and left behind on Mars. The movie centers on his struggles to survive and fellow astronauts' efforts to rescue him. Watney survives in part by growing potatoes in Martian soil enriched by human fertilizer.

Recently, Elon Musk, of Tesla automobile fame, is convinced that the survival of the human species may depend on space travel. Frustrated by NASA's lack of interest in manned space flight, Musk decided to spend $100 million of his own money to launch a company, SpaceX, with the purpose of taking people to space in his lifetime. Despite many setbacks, the company now has reusable rockets that regularly launch satellites or make trips to the International Space Station for NASA. The next goal is a Mars trip, though space industry veterans are skeptical.

Q49: *Is there evidence that the big bang really happened?*

I t's very hard to believe the whole universe emanated from a single, infinitely small point. How could that possibly be?

Up to around the 1950s, astronomers considered the universe to be infinite and ageless. Then in the middle of the 1900s, scientists discovered that objects in deep space were moving away from us, and away from one another. They found that every galaxy in the universe was moving away from every other galaxy. The more distant the galaxy, the faster it's moving away from us. This fits with Albert Einstein's 1936 prediction.

Galaxies seem to be moving away, and the space between galaxies is stretching. How do astrophysicists know this? We know the galaxies are moving away because of an effect called redshift, like the way that a car sounds more high-pitched as it approaches you, and more low-pitched as it moves away. It is known as the Doppler effect.

To see how this might be possible, try the following exercise. Blow up a balloon to about half its maximum size. Use a marker to make several ink spots on the balloon. Five or six ought to do. Now continue blowing up the balloon, keeping your eye on the spots. Do you see that every spot is moving away from every other spot?

A logical conclusion is that at some time in the past the galaxies must have been closer together, indeed much closer together. At some point in space and time, every single piece of matter in the universe must have been squished together into an unthinkably tiny point.

There is another intriguing and convincing bit of evidence of the big bang theory. The big bang theory says that in the first few moments after the expansion started, the universe should be incredibly hot. A pure white blinding light from radiation would have disintegrated us, if we were around, in an instant.

After about 13.8 plus billion years, there should be leftover evidence, a dull glow visible in every part of the universe. Scientists went looking for it and found it in 1965. It is called the Cosmic Microwave Background. It's the best evidence we have that the big bang really happened.

Did space or time exist prior to the big bang? Most scientists would answer "no" to this question. The big bang marks the beginning of space and time as we know them. Stephen Hawking has said that asking what happened before the big bang is like asking what's north of the North Pole. The question doesn't really make sense.

The big bang was not really an explosion, since there was no air to carry any vibrations. The first particles to appear were quarks and leptons. The early universe was changing quickly as it expanded and cooled. Neutrons formed and then decayed into protons, and the first atoms of hydrogen were formed. Incredibly hot at more than 18 billion°F (10 billion°C), hydrogen gas clumped together, and under gravity, formed stars and galaxies.

Q50: *Why does the earth spin?*

T he solar system started out around 4.5 billion years ago as a vast cloud of dust and gas. As the cloud began to collapse under its own gravity, it flattened into a giant disk that rotated faster and faster, just like an ice skater who spins faster as she brings her arms in.

As the solar system spun with increased rotation rate, the sun formed at the center of a huge bulge, and the remaining swirling dust and gas clumped together to produce the planets, moons, asteroids, and some comets. As the planets formed, they kept this spinning motion. The spinning objects are nearly in the same plane and spin in the same direction. Looking down on Earth from above the North Pole, this spin would be in a counterclockwise direction.

That initial spin continues because there is no force to stop it. The fancy term for the phenomenon is conservation of angular momentum. Astronomers see that same mechanism throughout the universe in the shaping of galaxies and other solar systems.

While all that formation was going on, clumps of material were colliding, sideswiping each other, knocking off other pieces and setting them spinning also. The gravitational pull of big objects would capture smaller ones. Scientists believe this is how many planets acquired moons. There's a ton of chaos going on.

Scientists believe that during the formation of the solar system, a large object about the size of Mars impacted our young planet, knocking out a chunk that eventually became our moon.

That's not the only theory, but is the most reasonable idea based on examination of moon rocks brought back by the Apollo astronauts from 1969 to 1972.

Each planet has its own rotation rate, the time it takes to make one spin on its axis. For Earth, of course, the time is close to 24 hours. Mercury, the planet closest to the sun, needs 59 of our Earth days to make one spin. Venus takes 243 Earth days to make one rotation, and oddly, it rotates backward (clockwise) compared to the other planets. It requires 225 of our Earth days for Venus to go around the sun, making its day longer than its year. Now that is really odd!

Earth's 24-hour rotation rate is ideal for life. Earth can stay a comfortable temperature bathed in sunlight during the day and darkness at night. There are no extremes between day and night temps. Mercury, with its 59-Earth-day rotation, would not be acceptable, with a boiling hot sun for weeks at a time, then bitter cold for weeks at a time.

Living on Venus is out of the question. Covered by dense carbon dioxide clouds dripping killing sulfuric acid, Venus is about 850°F (450°C), about the temperature of a pizza oven.

Mars, with a very thin atmosphere of mostly carbon dioxide, provides a possibly livable climate. The Mars day is about the same length as Earth's, just a half hour longer. Being further from the sun, Mars is much colder, and there are no trees to start a fire, and no oxygen to help the fire burn. And no food and no vegetation, and bombarded with radiation. How about we just continue to make Earth more livable?

At one time, the moon was much closer to us than it is today. The moon's gravity causes the oceans to rise and fall, the tides as we know them. That friction between water and land causes the rotation of the earth to slow down, making each day a tiny bit longer and causing the moon to drift away from us. Even a spinning ice skater slows down eventually.

The length of our Earth day is increasing by 1.7 milliseconds per century. A millisecond is one thousandth of a second. The moon is moving away from us 1.5 inches (3.8 centimeters) per year. Hardly enough to notice.

Q51: *Why does Earth have air, when other planets don't?*

It turns out that other planets do have atmospheres, but not like ours on Earth. Some planets, such as the gas giants of Jupiter, Saturn, Uranus, and Neptune, have atmospheres. Venus, a planet just a bit smaller than Earth, has a very dense carbon dioxide atmosphere. Mars has a very thin, tenuous carbon dioxide atmosphere, and Mercury has no atmosphere at all. Also, there is no atmosphere on the moon.

A planet must have enough gravity to keep an atmosphere in place. Mercury and the moon are too small to retain an atmosphere. A planet's gravity depends on its mass; more mass, more gravity. A massive planet, such as the four gas giants, has enough gravity to hold onto a lot of gas molecules, such as hydrogen, helium, methane, and ammonia. But they are the wrong kinds of gas molecules to keep humans alive.

No planet in our solar system has an atmosphere containing an appreciable amount of oxygen—at least not the amount of oxygen needed to sustain life, or the kind of life we know here on Earth.

Earth's atmosphere today is made of 78 percent nitrogen, 21 percent oxygen, and about one percent various inert gases. But oddly enough, Earth's atmosphere started out with hardly any oxygen. Earth's original atmosphere was probably just hydrogen and helium, because those were the main gases in the dusty, gassy disk around the sun from which the planets formed. Earth and its atmosphere were very hot. Molecules of hydrogen and helium move really fast, especially when warm. In fact, they moved so fast they eventually all escaped Earth's gravity and drifted off into space.

Earth's remaining atmosphere was primarily carbon dioxide. Some oxygen was delivered as ice via comets during the early earth formation stage. But the real clue to oxygen on Earth is the emergence of life.

Volcanoes erupting on Earth, and comets and asteroids hitting Earth, gradually caused changes on our planet. Chemical reactions of simple organic compounds slowly led to the creation of amino acids, RNA, DNA and eventually self-replicating life-forms. That is the view of most scientists.

Some of those early life-forms of bacteria (prokaryotes) released oxygen as a waste product. Prokaryotes are microscopic single-celled organism that have neither a distinct nucleus nor other specialized organelles. Prokaryotes include bacteria. When these bacteria grew and multiplied, some of them processed carbon dioxide into sugars, with oxygen as a by-product. Gradually, the percentage of oxygen on Earth increased. More sophisticated life-forms emerged, including blue-green algae. About 70 percent of the oxygen in our air came from marine algae, and amazingly, we can't even see the algae because they are too small.

Life began to produce oxygen an estimated 2.7 billion years ago, which is about half the age of the earth and solar system. Before that time, methane-producing organisms had dominated Earth, but as Earth changed, so did life. As volcanic activity on Earth decreased, less nickel poured into the air. This sudden lack of nickel due to much less volcanic activity killed off methane producers.

Earth's crust cooled, allowing more oxygen-producing life-forms, such as algae, to appear. Algae and other life-forms that release oxygen during photosynthesis grew and took over, increasing the oxygen content of our atmosphere. Scientists refer to it as the Great Oxidation Event.

On Earth today, carbon dioxide gets converted into oxygen gas via photosynthesis. Plants give off oxygen, while we humans plus animals take in oxygen and give off carbon dioxide. The atmosphere upon which life depends was created by life itself, working to balance these two vital gases in our atmosphere. It has been a win-win situation for the whole planet!

It's clear our Earth once had a very different atmosphere compared to what we know today. Some of what we know about Earth's atmosphere in ancient history is locked in fossils, in sea bed drillings, in rock formations, and in vegetation.

Our fragile atmosphere did not come with an instruction book. We must learn all we can about it and protect it from harm.

Chapter Six

Art, Music, Sports and Math

Q52: *How do they put the lead in pencils?*

I t is truly amazing how much science and history is behind the lowly pencil. Even with the computer at center stage in the information age, there are 14 billion pencils sharpened every year. That's more than two pencils for every human walking the earth.

First off, it is graphite, not lead, that is put in pencils. The graphite is ground into a fine powder, then mixed with clay and water, and finally pressed together at high temperatures. The long, thin, rods of graphite are ready to go into "lead" pencils.

Early pencils were made by drilling a hole down a shaft of wood and sliding in a piece of lead. The Italians came up with that idea. That's not how pencils are made today. The English came up with the more modern method. A clue can be found by looking at the writing end of a brand-new wooden pencil before you sharpen it.

A machine cuts a lengthwise groove into a cedar wood rod. The depth of the grooved cut is half as deep as the graphite rod is thick. The lead rod is placed in the groove and a second grooved rod is placed and glued on top of the first. After the glue is dried, a machine sands down the glued joints and sends the pencil on to the painting machine. If you look at the end of a new pencil, you can see that line where the two halves were joined. Most pencil manufacturers make eight pencil lengths before a machine cuts them.

Each pencil has a shoulder cut on one end to allow for a metal ferrule to be secured onto the wood. A rubber plug is then inserted into the ferrule for an eraser on the end of the pencil. Some logo or trademark is stamped on the side.

We are familiar with the instructions to "Use a #2 pencil to fill in responses" in those bubble tests. The number printed on the side indicates the hardness of the graphite. The higher the number, the harder the graphite. A #2 is about right, because a

#3 pencil would leave a fainter mark that machines might not be able to read, and a #1 pencil might smudge or smear. The clay content determines the hardness—the more clay, the harder the pencil.

Graphite is a form of carbon. President Franklin Pierce had a graphite mine, an old historic mine in New Hampshire. Graphite from President Pierce's mine was used to make pencils. In 1849, the mine produced 20 tons (18 metric tons) of graphite per year at 3 to 5 cents per pound, or about $1,600 per year.

Finer crystals of graphite are often used in electrical components, as graphite is the only conductor of electricity that is not metallic in origin.

Graphite is used in batteries, including the newer lithium-ion ones. It's also used in making steel, brake linings on cars and trucks, and brushes in electric motors. Fiber graphite composites can be found in fishing rods, golf club shafts, pool cue sticks, bicycle frames, sports car body panels, and the fuselage of the Boeing 787 Dreamliner.

In 2016, in Nomi, Japan, architects unveiled a four-story seismic reinforcement building made completely of carbon fiber material.

Q53: Why are pencils yellow?

The best graphite in the world came from China during the 1890s. The Chinese associated the color yellow with excellence, royalty, and respect. Manufacturers in the United States and Europe wanted a way to tell people that their pencils were the best. The European and American company Koh-I-Noor was the first to paint pencils yellow, and yellow became linked with high quality in the minds of users. Any other color was just inferior. Painting something yellow was associated with quality. That idea caught on with school buses, too.

Joseph Dixon developed a means to mass-produce pencils in 1870. He founded the Dixon Ticonderoga Company. Today, the Dixon Ticonderoga Wood-Cased Black Core #2 pencil, soft and yellow, is considered one of the finest pencils in the world. And yes, you can find it at big-box stores.

Early on, pencil makers used red cedar. It had a fine aromatic smell and did not splinter when sharpened. A fine-grained wood, cedar can withstand great variations in temperature and humidity, which is important, since pencils may be shipped all over the world. Today, pencils are made from incense cedar (*Calocedrus decurrens*), dyed and perfumed to look and smell like red cedar.

The Chinese use basswood. It's very lightweight, soft, has a fine-grained texture and is easy to work and shape. It's porous, allowing the wood to soak up paint.

Other countries paint their pencils different colors. German pencils are commonly green, blue, and black. France and Italy like dark red or black pencils with yellow lines. Australian pencils are typically red with black bands on one end.

Ben Franklin had pencils for sale in 1729 at his newspaper, the *Pennsylvania Gazette*. George Washington used a 3-inch (7.6-centimeter) long pencil when he was surveying the Ohio area in the early 1760s. Henry David Thoreau's father had a pencil factory in Concord, New Hampshire. John Steinbeck used 300 pencils to write *East of Eden*. Johnny Carson played with a pencil when interviewing guests and between guests. The pencil was just a prop. He never wrote anything. To avoid accidents, both ends of his pencil had erasers.

Getting a new pencil as a kid was a real treat for me, attending a one-room country school out on Oak Grove Ridge in the middle of Crawford County, Wisconsin. On one occasion, when I was about eight years old, I got a new pencil that, when sharpened, showed lead (actually graphite) on one side of the point, but left a lot of wood on the other side of the point. My dad explained that the pencil maker did not have the lead centered in the middle of the pencil. How could my dad have figured that out, I wondered? I thought my dad was just about the smartest man in the world.

Q54: *How are things colorful all around us?*

A question with some beautiful complexity. Color itself isn't a thing we can touch, like a table or coffee cup. Rather, color is how our eyes interpret reflection of light off certain objects. That's why we don't see colors in the dark; there's no light to reflect. To understand color, we must consider two processes: how light interacts with matter and how human perception works.

First, how light interacts with matter. White light, the kind of light from the sun, or from an incandescent or fluorescent lightbulb, is made up of a range of waves of different lengths. These waves are just like water waves but much too short for us to see as individual waves.

Everything is made of atoms, and each atom has a different electron configuration. When light hits objects, some is absorbed by the material and some is reflected. Which waves are reflected and which are absorbed is determined by the match between the incoming light frequency and the natural vibration frequency of the electrons in the given material.

This is the part that can get complex but it goes to the heart of why, for example, a car is red or a car is blue. It gets right down to the atomic level. The interaction between the light frequency and vibration frequency of the material also explains whether an object is opaque or transparent.

When we see something that has, say, a red color, that's because light of a very narrow range of wavelengths is reflected to our eye more strongly than light of other wavelengths.

What about human perception? In the back of the eye is the retina, which acts much like the film in a camera. The retina is covered by millions of light-sensitive cells, some shaped like rods and some like cones. The rods are found on the edges or periphery of the retina and are sensitive to black-and-white and dimly lit objects. The cones are concentrated in the center of the retina and pick up color and brightly lit objects.

Those specialized center cones are sensitive to the three primary colors of red, green, and blue light. When we see a red rose, we know that the cones sensitive to red light have been stimulated and sent electrical impulses via the optic nerve to the visual cortex of the brain. When we see a yellow banana, both the red and green cone receptors have been stimulated. If we're looking at white snow, all three types of cone receptors have been jolted, as red, green, and blue make up white.

The human eye is most sensitive to the yellow-green color, the same color as crossing guard vests, construction worker jackets, girls' team softballs, and school and pedestrian crossing signs.

Dogs, cats, and most other animals have extremely poor color vision. They see mostly grays. Bees and butterflies and some birds can see in the ultraviolet range, an area that humans can't. Bees need ultraviolet vision to identify targets to pollinate. Flower petals scatter ultraviolet light, allowing bees to zero in on their target.

Historically, it was Isaac Newton, in the early 1670s, who realized that color was not inherent in objects, but rather that the surfaces of objects reflect some colors and absorb all the others. We perceive only the reflected colors. Newton knew that the three primary colors for light were red, green, and blue. He also hinted that the primary colors for paints and pigments were different from those for light. Today, we call those primary colors magenta, yellow, and cyan.

Q55: Why do you move your hand back when you catch a hard-thrown baseball?

$\bullet\ \bullet$

I f you catch a hard-hit or hard-thrown baseball with your arm held stiffly, it can hurt. In this case, the baseball is brought to zero velocity in a very short distance and time. Newton's laws come into play in this situation, namely the second and third laws. Newton's second law is $F = ma$. F is for force, m means mass, and the letter a stands for acceleration, which means a change in velocity. To stop the ball, a large negative acceleration must be applied to the ball. That implies a large force.

Newton's third law states that a large force of the ball on the hand (action), must be accompanied by a large force of the hand on the ball (reaction). That's the source of the pain.

To lessen the sting, move your hand backward in the direction the ball is going. The ball is brought to zero velocity over a period of time and distance. The resulting acceleration is much lower, with a much gentler force on the catching hand.

This slowing technique is witnessed at picnics and family reunions in the egg-throwing contests. The two winners are those who can toss an egg with the greatest distance between them, catch the egg, and not have it break. If the egg is caught with a stiff arm, the egg will not survive. Winning contestants move their cupped hands backward just as the egg is to be caught. They are increasing the time and distance the egg takes to come to a halt.

Another noteworthy example is evident when people jump off a table or ledge at a height of about 1 to 4 feet (30.5 to 121.9 centimeters). People bend their knees upon landing. The bulk of the body is brought to rest over a larger distance, imparting much less force to the legs. Failure to bend the knees will make the body come to a stop in a short distance and time, resulting in painful injuries to hips, knees, ankles, and back.

Let's throw in, at no charge, a physics equation called the Impulse-Momentum Theorem. Here's the equation: $Ft = mv$. The Ft is impulse, and we can express it as force multiplied by the change in time. The mv side is stated as momentum multiplied by the change in velocity.

When the ball is thrown very hard, the right-hand side of the equation (mv) is a constant. The total is just the mass of the baseball times the velocity of the baseball. You, as the baseball catcher, can't change that.

Remember, whatever is on the right side (mv) is equal to whatever is on the left side (Ft). But you, as the smart baseball catcher, realize that you have some control of those two variables, force and time. If you can increase the time, by bringing your hand back as you catch the ball, then the force of the ball on your hand (and the resulting pain) goes down.

The whole concept of cushioning is widespread in everyday life. We see instances wherever we look. Examples include seat belts, air bags, highway breakaway barriers, running shoes, and padding in football helmets.

Q56: Are today's baseballs "juiced up"?
. . . .

Justin Verlander, ace player for the Houston Astros, has stated publicly that he believes they are. After just five World Series games in 2017, there had been 22 home runs, with 8 homers in Game Two and 7 homers in Game Five.

Houston Astro pitcher Dallas Keuchel was quoted as saying after Game Two, "Obviously, the balls are juiced." He claimed that Major League Baseball had doctored the baseballs to make sure the games would be more exciting and people would stick around, since anything might happen in one swing.

Others aren't so sure. Los Angeles Dodger three-time Cy Young winner, Clayton Kershaw, says, "I don't really pay attention to it. I just assume that both sides are dealing with it, so I'm not going to worry about it."

Dodgers reliever Brandon Morrow, after giving up two homers in Game Five, claimed, "I haven't personally noticed anything. I haven't tried to think about it either, it's not something you want to put in your own head."

Conspiracy theorists do have something to go on. Baseball Commissioner Robert Manfred declared right after the 2015 All Star game, "The fans love homers."

Not all changes in baseball favor the batter. Over the years, the strike zone was increased in size, favoring the pitcher. At the beginning of the 2015 season, MLB realized that the game was on life support. Fans love offense, and they weren't seeing it. On the day he became commissioner in January 2015, Manfred said, "I'm cognizant of the drop in offense over the last five years, and it's become a topic of conversation in the game, and it's something that we're going to have to continue to monitor and study."

Offense started rebounding during the second half of the 2015 season. And in 2017, a record 6,105 home runs were hit, a 2.4 percent increase from the previous mark of 5,963 set in 2000 at the height of the steroids era. "They took the juice out of players, and now they want to put the juice in baseballs," declared one baseball writer.

Baseball production and testing is very stringent. The engineering lab at the University of Massachusetts at Lowell has the contract to test Major League baseballs. The coefficient of restitution (COR) is a measure of how bouncy a ball is. The COR gives the ratio of how far a ball bounces back to how far it is dropped. A Major League ball must have a COR between 0.514 and 0.578.

Balls tested this past year averaged 0.55, toward the upper end of allowable "bounciness." After reviewing the university's findings, Major League Baseball said the tests verified that this year's baseballs were in line with its specifications.

A ball put in play must also be a certain weight, 5.125 ounces (145.3 grams), plus or minus 0.125 ounce (3.5 grams). It must have a certain circumference, 9.125 inches (23.2 centimeters), plus or minus 0.125 inch (0.3 centimeters). It would be very difficult to cheat on the dimensions. Anybody with a scale and tape in the dugout could measure the baseball.

There is anecdotal evidence that something else could be going on here. The rules (MLB 4.01c) say that the home club supplies the baseballs, while the umpire inspects the baseballs and ensures they are regulation baseballs and that they are properly rubbed to remove the gloss.

Before all major league games, an umpire or clubhouse attendant rubs six dozen or more balls with mud to give them a rougher surface, making them easier for pitchers to grip. The mud comes from the Delaware River, on the New Jersey side. That's the same river that General Washington crossed with his troops across on December 25, 1776, to surprise and capture the Hessian soldiers working for the British. The rubbing mud's unique feature is that it is "very fine, like thick chocolate pudding," and it has been considered the "perfect baseball-rubbing mud." The minerals make it like a fine-grit sandpaper. It buffs the gloss off the ball without damaging the leather.

Baseball writer Rob Arthur mentioned slicker baseballs in his study from this summer as well. A slicker ball moves through the air differently. A slicker baseball moves faster toward home plate, which also means it's going to go faster heading back in the other direction after being hit.

A number of players and researchers have mentioned that the baseballs used today are slicker than they were in the past. Players participating in the World Series claim the slicker ball causes sliders to flatten out. The slider is one of the most effective pitches in the game. Ted Williams once called the slider "the best pitch in baseball."

The slider is a sharp-breaking pitch that the pitcher uses to set up his fastball. The pitcher throws a fastball, then throws a slider right after it, in the same spot that he previously has thrown the fastball. The batter can't tell it is a slider; it looks just like a fastball, but a tad slower. The slider breaks down and away from a right-hand batter.

Sports Illustrated quoted the two 2017 World Series pitching coaches, Houston Astros' Brent Strom and the Dodgers' Rick Honeycutt, saying the slickness of the ball made throwing sliders difficult. The slicker balls may account for a rise in pitcher blisters, an affliction that has struck Dodger pitcher Rich Hill, a few times in the past couple of seasons. Other pitchers have joined the blister brigade, including Corey Kluber, Noah Syndergaard, Jake Arrieta, Johnny Cueto, and David Price, and Marcus Stroman.

Stroman's Toronto Blue Jay teammate, Aaron Sanchez, who has been sidelined by blisters for parts of the last two seasons, complained about a blister "epidemic" in baseball. A few players believe the stitches are higher, causing more finger-on-baseball friction.

Commissioner Rob Manfred has the last word. He insists nothing nefarious is going on. "I'm absolutely confident that the balls that we're using are within our established specifications."

Q57: *What is calculus, anyway?*

Calculus is the mathematical study of change. There are two main branches of calculus. Integration deals with accumulation, areas, and volumes. Differential calculus concerns derivatives, or rate of change.

Calculus is the mathematical language of scientists, economists, and engineers. Calculus can solve many problems that algebra cannot. Let's take this example. Say a faucet starts pouring a 5 percent saltwater solution into a 20-gallon bucket at a rate of 1 gallon per minute. The bucket starts with a 9 percent saltwater solution and is draining the contents at 2 gallons per minute. How much water is in the bucket and what is the salt content after two minutes? It is difficult for algebra to solve this problem, especially if the flow rate of either intake or discharge is changing, but calculus can.

Another example: A fellow is pushing a crate along an incline from the ground up to the back of a truck. If the board incline is straight, algebra can calculate the work (energy) needed to accomplish the task. But if the incline is swayed or curved, calculus is needed.

Physics makes particular use of calculus for Newton's laws of motion, electricity, and magnetism. Electrical engineers use integration to determine the length of power cables between two substations that are miles apart. The cable, hung from poles, is constantly curving. Calculus enables the engineers to figure out the exact length of cable. In medicine, calculus is used to find the optimal branching angle of a blood vessel to maximize flow. It is used to develop dosing laws, figure out the elimination rate of drugs from the body, or develop models of radiation to target tumors. Credit card companies utilize calculus to set the minimum payments due by taking into account changing interest rates and changing available balances. Auto engineers use calculus to find the center of mass of SUVs so they can stay within the limits of federal specifications for safety. NASA depends on calculus for planning space missions, especially deep space missions that have varying orbital velocities and gravitational influences of the sun and moon. Biologists use calculus to determine the rate of growth of a bacterial culture when there are multiple variables, such as temperature, light, and food source. Graphic artists use calculus in constructing, changing, and viewing three-dimensional models, as in all those computer programs we see manipulating scenes for planning a kitchen space, or landscaping, or building construction. Architects use calculus to determine the amount of material in a domed stadium and to calculate the weight of the dome and type of support structure needed.

There is hardly any aspect of modern life in which calculus is not used. Universities, military, airlines, construction companies, the entertainment industry . . . they all use calculus.

They say that "necessity is the mother of invention." And so it was with calculus. Isaac Newton needed the principles of calculus to explain his laws of motion, planetary motion, gravitation, and fluid flow. He explained those concepts in his 1687 tome *Principles of Mathematics.*

At the same time, Gottfried Wilhelm Leibniz in Germany published his notion of the calculus. A bitter argument broke out between the two over who was the originator of the calculus. The Englishman, Isaac Newton, a rather quarrelsome bloke, accused the exceedingly pushy German Leibniz of plagiarism. Apparently, Newton had shared his notes with members of the Royal Society who then talked to some German friends over a few ales.

Historians have looked over all the notes and papers of both Newton and Leibniz and concluded that they both developed calculus independently. Newton was the first to apply calculus to general physics, and Leibnitz spent much time on the formalism and symbols of calculus.

Q58: *What is a Fermi question?*
· ·

H ere are some Fermi questions: Car tires wear down, so how many atoms are lost in each rotation of a car tire on the road? How many hairs are there on a human head? What is the volume of human blood in the world? How many drops of water are there in Lake Erie? How large a collision is needed to split the moon in half? How much electrical power does the United States use per year? How many piano tuners are there in New York City?

A Fermi question requires an estimation of physical quantities to arrive at an answer that is at least within a power of 10—in other words, an estimate that falls between 10 times too little and 10 times too much. The goal of a Fermi question is get an answer by making reasonable assumptions about the situation, not necessarily by coming up with an exact answer.

Fermi Questions are one of the events in Science Olympiads held in high schools across America and in many foreign countries. The process requires students to ask many more questions to arrive at a best estimate. The team must rely on open communication between its members, estimation abilities, and math skills. A Fermi question emphasizes process rather than "the answer," because some answers are almost impossible to come by.

Take, for example, the question "How many drops of water are there in Lake Erie?" Approaching this question requires an estimate of the volume of a drop of water, estimating the volume of Lake Erie from its approximate dimensions, and converting units to yield an answer.

Enrico Fermi (1901–1954) is one of my favorite scientists. Fermi was an Italian physicist best known for his contributions to nuclear physics and the development of quantum theory. He combined a probing, questioning mind with intense personal drive. He was always looking for a new challenge, be it skiing, mountain climbing, or swimming. Fermi has been called the last of the double-threat scientists. He combined a brain that conceived wonderful elegant theories to explain nature with a pair of hands that built and operated impressive laboratory experiments.

In 1938, Fermi earned a Nobel Prize in Physics for his work on the nuclear process. He was also awarded several patents on the use of nuclear power. Shortly afterward, he fled Mussolini's Italy because his wife, Laura, was Jewish. Fermi and his family settled in the United States, first at Columbia University and then later at the University of Chicago.

Fermi led the team that designed and built the crude nuclear reactor that obtained the first artificial self-sustaining nuclear chain reaction on December 2, 1942. During World War II, he was a member of the Manhattan Project team that developed the atomic bomb at Los Alamos, New Mexico.

In the early morning hours of July 16, 1945, the atomic scientists gathered at Trinity site, in the desert near Alamogordo, New Mexico. They huddled behind bunkers 5 miles (8 kilometers) from the windmill-like platform atop which sat the world's first atomic bomb. To safely view the blinding explosion, scientists were issued welders' glasses. Seconds after the blinding flash, a pressure shock wave swept by the observers.

Enrico Fermi grabbed a handful of sand and tossed it in the air as the shockwave passed. Based on the distance the sand was swept downwind, Fermi estimated the yield of the first atomic bomb to be about 20,000 tons (18,000 metric tons) of TNT. Fermi's reputation is cemented.

Q59: What are some of the most common science questions that kids ask?

A recent survey in both the United States and England found that the five most often asked science questions from kids were: Why is the moon out during the daytime? Why is the sky blue? Will we discover aliens? How much does the earth weigh? How do airplanes stay up?

About two thirds of the parents surveyed said they struggled with the answers. 20 percent admitted that if they didn't know the answer, they made up an explanation or said that no one knows. Let's tackle several of these questions.

Why is the moon out during the daytime? The moon is visible as many hours during the day as it is visible at night. To be visible, the moon must be above the horizon. On average, the moon is above the horizon for 12 hours out of every 24. The moon can be seen during the day nearly every day, except for when it's close to a new moon or a full moon. The best times of the month to see the moon during daytime hours are during the first and third quarters. That's when the moon is 90 degrees away from the sun in the sky. Most any calendar will show the phases of the moon.

Why is the sky blue? Light, traveling as a wave, comes from the sun and is made of many colors. Each wavelength is associated with a different color. The colors can be remembered as ROYGBIV (red, orange, yellow, green, blue, indigo, and violet). Red, orange, and yellow have long wavelengths and the blue, indigo, and violets have a shorter wavelength. Green is in the middle.

When light from the sun passes through our atmosphere, it runs into molecules of moisture, water droplets, dust, smoke, and other particulate matter. The size of these particles is closest to the size of the shorter wavelengths, which are the BIV, or blue, indigo, and violet colors. So those waves are scattered the most.

That means the blue is reflecting and ricocheting all over the place, including to the ground and our eyes. A logical question: Indigo and violet are shorter than blue, so why don't we see indigo and violet? Answer: Our eyes are more sensitive to blue, and not very sensitive to indigo and violet.

Will we find aliens? There's no telling if people on Earth will ever discover any alien life in the universe. SETI (Search for Extra Terrestrial Intelligence) Institute scientists are fairly confident that we will find something in the next 20 years. They base their guesstimate on improved technology in radio telescopes that scan the heavens, plus the rapid pace in discovering planets suitable for life. I do believe the 20-year figure is way too optimistic.

How much does the earth weigh? Kind of a tricky question and it can be answered in two different ways.

First, the earth doesn't weigh anything because it is in free-fall around the sun. It's the same reason the astronauts "float." They are technically in free fall all the way around the earth. If they step on a scale in space, the scale would read zero, because the scale is also in free-fall. If you or I jumped from a building while standing on a scale on the way down, the scale would read zero. The only difference between jumping from a building and the astronauts in space is that the astronauts are moving forward, at a speed of 5 miles (8 kilometers) per second, at the same time they are in free fall.

However, if we look at the mass of the earth, that is a different story. Mass is not dependent on an object's position in space. It is basically "how much stuff there is." The mass of the earth is about 1.3 times 10 to the 25th power pounds. Make that 1.3 and add 25 zeros on the end. Or 100 million billion *Titanics*.

I believe the second answer is what most people want to know. If you could pick up the earth and put it on a scale, what would the scale read?

Q60: What is the science and mathematics behind musical instruments?

M usic from instruments is produced by vibrating strings, vibrating air columns, or percussion. Much of what we know about the science of vibrating strings can be traced back to the Greek philosopher Pythagoras (about 500 BCE). He found that if one string vibrates with twice the frequency of an identical string, we hear the higher frequency as one octave higher in pitch than the lower frequency. An octave difference is either twice the pitch or half the pitch.

One can demonstrate this by striking the middle C on a piano, then the next C to the right. The new C will be one octave higher (twice the pitch) and the second C will resonate with the middle C and increase its loudness.

Pythagoras also found that a whole number ratio of frequencies produces sounds that are harmonious to the ear. The musical scale is based on the frequency ratio of sounds. Pitch represents the perceived fundamental frequency of a sound—the frequency of vibration that produces a musical note. Intuitively, pitch refers to the highness or lowness of notes in the music. We can use the term *pitch* and *frequency* interchangeably.

Vibrating string instruments need help making a sound heard. A vibrating string produces very little sound. Most string instruments, such as the guitar, violin, and cello, require some kind of sounding board. It is called forced vibration and increases the amplitude or loudness of the sound.

String instruments are played by changing the lengths of the strings. To tune a string instrument, a musician adjusts the tension of the string. A guitar player can rapidly move his or her fingers up and down the neck, pressing the string against the frets and hence changing the length of the string. Trying to play a stringed instrument by changing the tension would simply take too much time.

Woodwind instruments (clarinet, saxophone, flute, oboe, bassoon) and brass instruments (trombone, trumpet, tuba, French horn, cornet, pipe organ) produce music by utilizing a vibrating air column. Various valves make the air column longer or shorter. The shorter the air column, the higher the pitch or frequency.

Percussion instruments produce sounds in various ways. To create a drum, a material is stretched over a hollow container. The membrane vibrates when struck by a stick, mallet, or the hand. Xylophones employ vibrating bars of various lengths of metal or wood. Same with the glockenspiel. The lengths of the bars produce varying pitches. Each bar is tuned to a pitch on the musical scale. A short bar creates a high pitch and a longer bar generates a lower pitch. Cymbals are clanging metal discs.

The piano is an interesting case. Most people consider the piano to be a percussion instrument because the strings are set into motion or vibration by a hammer, which acts on the bridge of the piano, which causes the sounding board to vibrate. However, the sound itself is produced by vibrating strings.

Q61: Why do bottles make a noise when you blow over them?

Bottles, such as pop bottles, ketchup bottles, and wine bottles, make that noise for the same reason that church pipe organs work—namely the phenomenon of resonance. The bottle becomes a pipe whose length is determined by how much soda or water is in the bottle. There is a formula or equation that determines the note or pitch you hear. Basically, the wavelength of the sound is four times the length of the closed pipe (pop bottle).

There is a formula that relates the main three properties of any wave. The three properties are wavelength, wave velocity or speed, and frequency. Frequency and pitch mean the same, which is the number of vibrations per second. The formula states that the wavelength is equal to the velocity divided by the frequency.

A 12-inch (30.5-centimeter)-long pop bottle will produce a pitch or note of about 262 Hz, which is middle C on the piano keyboard. The longer the bottle or organ pipe, the lower the note, pitch, or frequency of the sound.

There are basically three ways to get sound from a pop bottle. One way is to blow across the top, as mentioned above. Another is to rap the bottle. Hold the blade of a heavy table knife and rap the handle against the bottle. The pitch or note you get depends on how much water is in the bottle. But the results are opposite of blowing across the top. In other words, the more water the pop bottle contains, the lower the pitch. That's because there is more mass, and something with more mass will vibrate at a lower pitch.

St. Luke's Bottle Band, based in Park Ridge, Illinois, has performed on America's Got Talent and National Public Radio, and gives concerts all around the United States. They are a real treat to watch and hear. Check out their videos on YouTube. Some members of the Bottle Band blow across the top, some rap with a metal mallet, and some hook a finger in the opening and sort of "pluck" it. With different size bottles and varying amounts of water, most all pitches or frequencies are produced. They are a big hit and have a wonderful sound!

Every year on the busy sidewalks of Copenhagen, a group of Danish students play traditional Christmas carols using taped-together beer bottles. They delight large groups of bystanders.

Chapter Seven

Incredible Technology

Q62: *What are the top 10 engineering feats of the last 50 years?*

. . . .

At a recent meeting of the National Academy of Engineers, 1,500 members were polled on what they thought were the top 10 engineering feats of the last 50 years.

On almost everyone's list was the Apollo landing and Neil Armstrong's walk on the moon in 1969. These engineers rated our going to the moon right up there with building the Panama Canal or the Egyptian pyramids. The array of scientific information, basic research and development, and product spin-off from the Apollo program has returned an estimated tenfold on our investment. Here is the entire list of the top 10:

1. Apollo landing on the moon

2. Laser

3. Optical fibers

4. Microprocessor

5. Genetic engineering

6. CAT scanner

7. Jumbo jet

8. Satellites

9. Advanced composite materials

10. CAD/CAM (computer-aided design/computer-aided manufacturing)

As we go move into the late 2010s, it's hard to imagine life without many of those top 10 inventions. They touch every facet of our life. Just look what microprocessors (computers) and satellites have done for business, industry, and communication via the Internet. Genetic engineering, the laser, and the CAT (computer-assisted tomography) scanner have revolutionized medicine.

Some feats, such as creating advanced composite materials, are often hidden from direct view, but show up in our products.

Others, like CAD/CAM (computer-assisted design/computer-assisted manufacturing), help make U.S. industries competitive with overseas companies. Try to imagine what the next 50 years will bring!

Q63: *Why do batteries die?*

B atteries do not contain electricity. They have the potential to make electricity by using the chemicals in the battery. The chemicals are kept apart until the battery is hooked up to some device to be powered. Then the chemicals react and produce a current flow or electricity.

Electrons are the outer part of all atoms. An electrical current is the flow of those electrons from one place to another. For this to happen, electrons must leave one atom and jump to another, like a frog on lily pads.

One atom must be willing to give up its electrons and another kind of atom must be willing to take it on. Some atoms hang onto their electrons more tightly than others. When two atoms can make a mutually beneficial deal, a chemical reaction takes place. It's called a redox reaction.

In a battery, the two groups of atoms are kept separate from each other, most often by a wet piece of paper. When a switch is closed and a circuit is completed, the electrons are ready to go to work. Now, instead of trying to pass across the paper barrier, the electrons can travel along the wire to join the other group of atoms.

This electron-passing game is what makes electricity, which is the movement or flow of electrons. A massive number of these electrons push their way through a one-way street called a circuit, which can light a bulb, toast some bread, or make a little pink bunny wander around beating a drum.

Zinc is one kind of atom that likes to pass electrons. Manganese is the kind of atom that's a receiver of electrons. In our most common batteries—AAA, AA, C, D, and 9-volt—the battery case is made of zinc, and a carbon rod down the center replaces manganese. The battery case is the negative terminal and the carbon rod is the positive terminal. When you put the battery in place, such as in a flashlight, metal contacts connect the positive and negative terminals, allowing electricity to flow.

Longer-lasting and more expensive batteries are the alkaline type. Duracell and Energizer brands are this variety. The electrodes are zinc and manganese, with an alkaline electrolyte. Other atoms that are good for batteries include lead, lithium, mercury, nickel, and cadmium.

Batteries die when the passer atoms have no more electrons to pass. The little pink bunny bangs the drum slowly, and then stops.

Some batteries are rechargeable, such as the lead acid battery in our cars. Electron flow is reversed and stored. Nickel cadmium (NiCad) batteries are another example. NiCads have gotten a bad rap because of the "memory effect." If the battery is continually recharged before it has discharged beyond 50 percent, it "forgets" it could be fully discharged to begin with. These batteries should be completely discharged every few weeks before being fully charged.

Nickel-metal hydrides are rechargeable and do not have the memory problem. Lots of these are going into laptop computers.

We'll be hearing a lot about lithium-air and lithium ion batteries powering electric cars. Lithium is soft, silver-white, and the lightest of all metals. Large amounts of it are extracted from briny or dried-up lakes in Bolivia, Argentina, and Chile. Lead, which is utilized in our common lead acid batteries, is one of the heaviest metals. Electric cars on the road today utilize lithium ion batteries.

Q64: How do lie detectors work?

A lie detector, often referred to as a polygraph machine, is a combination of three or four medical devices that monitor changes in the body. The body functions are heart rate, blood pressure, breathing (respiratory) rate, and galvanic skin resistance (sweatiness). The examiner is looking for changes in comparison to normal levels. The concept here is that a person who is being deceptive will have significant involuntary responses, reflecting the stress of lying.

An examiner connects several tubes and wires to the subject. Two air-filled rubber tubes (pneumographs) are placed around the person's chest. These tubes measure breathing rate. The tubes are connected to a bellows. The bellows is connected to mechanical arm, which is connected to an ink-filled pen that makes marks on a scrolling paper. As the suspected liar's chest expands and contracts, the pressure of the air in the tubes changes.

That's the analog kind you see in movies. Today's digital machines use a transducer to convert the amount of displaced air into an electronic signal.

Next, a blood pressure cuff is attached to the subject's upper arm. Tubes go from the cuff to the machine. Changes in blood pressure cause changes in the amount of air in the tubes, which are connected to bellows, now a transducer, and move a pen on the machine. The systolic (high number) and diastolic (low number) blood pressure are monitored, just as with the sphygmomanometer a doctor uses at the clinic or hospital.

Of course, this pressure cuff keeps track of heart rate at the same time. Heart rate is the number of beats per minute, usually around 72.

Galvanic skin resistance measures the skin's ability to conducts electricity. Skin conducts electricity much better when it is wet (sweaty) compared to when it is dry. We sweat more when under stress. The fingers are the most porous places on the human body, so they are a good place to pick up dampness from sweat. The examiner places electrodes on the subject's fingers. Some machines also detect arm and leg movement.

How good are lie detectors? They are not very good at all. Imagine you are asked to take a lie detector test. Think how intimidating that can be. All these tubes and wires hooked up and the examiner starts asking questions. A normal person may be afraid the machine will interpret a truthful response as a lie. The person might sweat, and the heart rate might rise. The person's nervousness will lead to what is called a false positive result.

On the other end, trained liars, like spies, can easily fool a lie detector. They use tacks placed in shoes, bite the tongue or lip, use sedatives, or put antiperspirants on their fingertips.

How good is the examiner? Lots of subjective judgment is involved in looking at the results of any lie detector test. Lie detectors are seldom admissible in court, especially in local and state courts. At the federal level, it is usually up to the judge involved.

Robert Hanssen was one of the FBI's most trusted agents. From roughly 1979 to 2001, Hanssen was a mole who sold the Russians our most vital secrets, in what has been described as "the worst intelligence disaster in U.S. history." When under investigation, Hanssen took a lie detector test and passed it. The 2007 movie *Breach* does a pretty good job of showing how he was finally caught. It does not go deeply into the tremendous damage he caused. Also, a 2002 made-for-television movie *Master Spy: The Robert Hanssen Story* is excellent. If interested, Google Robert Hanssen and see why he was given a 15 consecutive life sentences and sits in solitary in a federal prison near Florence, Colorado.

For more than 22 years, the FBI mole delivered to Moscow 6,000 pages of documents and 26 computer disks detailing the bureau's "sources and methods, including its latest techniques for electronic eavesdropping." As a counterintelligence expert at the FBI, Hanssen had unusually broad access to the bureau's files. He betrayed a number of operatives in Moscow who spied for the United States. Those spies were rounded up and executed.

Q65: How do telephones work?

The landline telephone is one of the most amazing devices we have in our house. Pick it up, push a few buttons, and you can talk to almost anyone on planet Earth. Compare that with 1815 when the Battle of New Orleans was fought between a hodgepodge of American irregulars and British redcoats several weeks after a peace treaty had been signed. Sure could have used a telephone back then!

The basic telephone has not changed in 100 years. A simple telephone would have a speaker (receiver) put up to our ear, a microphone near our lips, and a switch to connect and disconnect our telephone to the phone company.

The microphone that you speak into is really a little cup filled with carbon granules. A thin flexible sheet of metal is placed over the cup. An electric current is sent through the carbon granules. The sound waves from our voice press the granules together and change the amount of current that goes through the granules. Thus, our voice is changed to wobbles in an electric current that can be sent on to the telephone company.

The receiver is like any other speaker in our radio, television, or CD player. The speaker is an interaction between two magnetic fields. One magnet, really an electromagnet, is a coil of wire attached to a flexible diaphragm called a speaker cone. The other magnet is a permanent magnet, like the kind that holds papers on your refrigerator.

When an electric current goes through the coil of wire, it produces a magnetic field. This magnetic field interacts with the magnetic field from the permanent magnet, causing the cone to move back and forth, producing sound.

Some microphones use extremely thin metal sheets that bend a crystal. These piezoelectric crystals produce a voltage when flexed. The piezoelectric speakers work in much the same way.

A functioning telephone also has a keypad touch-tone for dialing. It has a bell or ringer to signal a call and a duplex coil, so the speaker doesn't hear his or her own voice. A pair of wires runs from the house to a junction box that sits beside a street or highway. The call goes to the phone company, where it is chopped up or digitized at 8,000 samples per second. The phone company can now send the conversation down a wire or fiber optic cable along with dozens of other callers. The phone continues to work even if the power or electricity to the house is cut off. The phone company sends the power right along the phone wires.

Why does a voice on a telephone sound different from the voice of the same person standing next to you? Phone companies cut off, or filter out, all tones, pitches, or frequencies below 400 hertz and above 3,400 hertz. Intelligible speech lies in the range between those values. We don't want to hear low pitches or bass frequencies because they don't help us understand speech. Higher frequencies are not needed. In addition, this way those smart phone company people can squeeze in more conversations on a single pair of wires.

Q66: How does a car engine work?
. . . .

I t's almost a miracle. A little more than 150 years ago, about the time of the Civil War, the fastest a human could travel was by horse. Wheels go back 5,500 years, and Egyptians had them on their chariots, but the chariots were pulled by horses. What was needed was an engine powering that chariot.

It's generally agreed that the credit for the first car goes to German engineer Karl Benz. In 1885, he fashioned a small gasoline engine to a three-wheeled cart. Benz needed a small compact engine. One was available. The first internal combustion engine had been invented by Nikolaus Otto in 1876, the centennial year of the United States and the year General Custer lost in southeastern Montana.

Most all cars today use a version of Otto's four-stroke internal combustion engine. When we say "internal combustion," we're talking about the "fire" or explosion being inside a cylinder, as opposed to outside as was normal in a steam engine. In a steam engine, fire below a closed chamber heated water inside that chamber, or boiler, to create steam, and the steam pressure drove a piston.

Car engines are converters that take the energy locked in gasoline and turn it into mechanical energy and heat. The mechanical energy becomes kinetic energy that drives the car forward. The main parts of the car engine are cylinders, valves, pistons, and crankshaft. Add a carburetor, a device that will mix about 16 parts air to one part of gasoline.

Think of a cylinder as an extra-strong paint can. A piston moves up and down in the cylinder. Two valves let stuff in and out of the cylinder. The intake valve allows a fine spray or mist of gasoline and air to enter the cylinder (intake stroke). The intake valve closes, and the piston moves to compress the mixture (compression stroke). A spark ignites the compressed gas, and the resulting mini-explosion pushes the piston (power stroke), which drives the crankshaft. The exhaust valve opens, and the spent gases are removed from the cylinder (exhaust stroke). The cycle is repeated.

The turning crankshaft is connected to the wheels through a series of devices called the transmission and drive train. The crankshaft also runs the valves that let gases in and out of the cylinders and such devices as an alternator, water pump, and the compressor for air-conditioning.

Most modern cars have either four or six cylinders. One of the characteristics of the four-stroke gasoline engine is that crankshaft must go around or rotate twice to get one powered push. The cylinder firings are designed so that they are out of step with each other. The power stroke is staggered so that one cylinder is always powering the crankshaft.

Cars, trucks, and motorcycles are a great convenience. They carry people and goods a great distance quickly and cheaply. But there is a downside. There are 1 billion cars on planet Earth, creating pollution and greenhouse gases (carbon dioxide). Also, gasoline comes from crude oil, which is a finite source that will eventually run out.

A logical question is: If gasoline has so many negatives attached to it, why do we still use gasoline or diesel fuel? Read on!

Q67: Why is gasoline such a good fuel for cars?

S hort answer: Gasoline is cheap, it's everywhere, and the infrastructure is in place to use it. From an engineering point of view (not considering environmental impact), gasoline is a very good fuel for the internal combustion engine. The internal combustion engine is the standard of the industry and has been for more than 100 years. However, that supremacy is being challenged by electric vehicles.

Gasoline and diesel fuel belong to a class of chemicals known as hydrocarbons. Coal, shale, wood, paper, and gases such as propane, methane, and butane are all hydrocarbons. As the name implies, hydrocarbons are made up of carbon molecules joined with a number of hydrogen molecules. When hydrocarbons are burned, the molecules split apart. The carbon and hydrogen combine with oxygen from the air to make carbon dioxide gas and water. The energy that held the molecules together is released as heat. And that process of combustion does release a lot of energy.

A huge advantage of gasoline is that it can be transported at normal temperatures and does not have to be pressurized. Gasoline does not need complex transport systems that are needed for liquefied natural gas (LNG) or liquid petroleum gas (LPG). Just pour gas in a tank and you're good to go. Safety is another factor. Liquid gasoline is quite hard to ignite.

When gasoline evaporates into a vapor, it becomes very explosive. That's exactly what you want in an engine and that is how engines work. Squirt some gasoline into a piston chamber as a mist or spray and add a spark. Boom, the air in the piston gets extremely hot, expands, and forces the piston to move. It's chemical energy to kinetic energy, the energy of motion.

Gasoline engines are only about 20 percent efficient, with 80 percent of the energy going into wasted heat and sound. But we don't seem to care, as gasoline is so cheap. For electric cars, the efficiency is close to 9 percent.

Why isn't more ethanol used in cars? Ethanol is OK, and it's used as a blend in many gasolines. But ethanol has some disadvantages that are not often discussed in the media. Ethanol provides much less energy per gallon than gasoline. A gallon of ethanol has about two thirds the energy of a gallon of gasoline.

Ethanol is hygroscopic, which means it absorbs water out of the air, and can damage engines due to too much water. Ethanol attacks seals and hoses in cars, so they need special design to resist deterioration. That is one reason car manufacturers resist using ethanol. They have flat-out stated that they will not honor any warranty if drivers use more than 10 percent ethanol in their fuel.

Another issue with ethanol is that it competes for land with food crops, mostly corn. That couples the price of food to the price of fuel, adding complexity to markets. It's costly to produce ethanol, taking as much energy to produce it as it provides. Seed costs, fertilizers, pesticides, refining costs—they all add up. It requires close to 1 gallon (3.8 liters) of fossil fuel to produce 1 gallon of ethanol. That is not much of a net gain. There are several other reasons why gasoline is so popular for cars. Gasoline has been around for a full century or more. The infrastructure is in place to drill for crude oil, refine crude oil to gasoline, and to transport gas to the customer. It's easy to find "filling stations" to deliver gas to the customer. It's hard to break that mold.

Still, our use of gasoline does cause problems for the planet. With more than 1 billion cars on the road, burning gasoline is sending huge amounts of carbon dioxide into the atmosphere. Carbon dioxide is a greenhouse gas. Light from the sun comes to the earth is short wavelengths and tries to leave in longer wavelengths, which are captured and re-emitted by greenhouse gases. The earth heats up. The same thing happens in a greenhouse. The area inside the glass of a greenhouse is heated up because the heat cannot escape the glass.

Our reliance on gasoline could be slowly changing. Electric cars are making deep inroads. Most every car manufacturer is putting one on the market. In 2017, 200,000 electric and hybrid vehicles were sold in the United States, and the numbers are rising. Elon Musk has committed to building electrical recharging stations across the country and the world. Meanwhile China, propelled by vast amounts of government money, has visions of dominating next-generation technologies. They are already the world's biggest supporters of electric cars. China has committed to having one fifth of its fleet run on alternative fuels by 2025. A Chinese official was recently quoted as saying that they would eventually do away with the internal combustion engine in new cars.

Q68: *What is the difference between E85 gas and biodiesel?*

E85 gasoline is a blend of 85 percent ethanol and 15 percent gasoline. Gasoline is refined from crude oil, but ethanol is alcohol produced from corn or sugar cane. Ethanol has a higher octane rating than regular gasoline.

Gasohol is a mixture of 90 percent gasoline and 10 percent ethanol. It has a slightly higher octane rating than regular gasoline. It can be burned in any car that uses regular gas. Sometimes it is a few cents a gallon cheaper than gasoline, and at other times, gasohol is a few cents more expensive. There is a lot of debate to the economics of producing ethanol. Much depends on the price of gasoline.

The octane rating or octane number is a standard measure of the performance of a fuel for an internal combustion engine. The higher the number, the more compression the fuel can withstand before igniting (detonating). The greater the compression, the more power the engine can deliver.

Either E85 or gasohol can be used in a flexible fuel vehicle (FFV). A FFV is a vehicle whose engine is set to run on gasoline and blends of gasoline and ethanol.

Biodiesel is biodegradable, burns cleanly, and is made from a renewable source. There are about 1,000 biodiesel stations across the United States. Biodiesel, which is made from soybeans, peanuts, canola, or animal fats, can be used full strength or blended with regular diesel fuel. Biodiesel is nontoxic and is fairly free of sulfur and cancer-causing benzene. It does slightly increase emissions of nitrogen dioxide. Nitrous dioxide is not kind to our ozone layer.

Biodiesel can be made from yellow grease, which is the byproduct of restaurant cooking oil. It can also be made from tallow, the fat that comes from cattle and sheep. Tallow is the same stuff that is used to make soap.

The big drawback to biodiesel is that it is not widely available. The most attractive customers are those that don't travel far, like construction vehicles that remain on site, or city buses and delivery trucks. The black-smoke-belching diesel city bus may be a thing of the past. Some National Parks, such as Yellowstone and Yosemite, are also using biodiesel. Many farmers and truck lines are using the blends B2, B5, and B20. The number represents the percentage of the fuel that is biodegradable.

Q69: Is a new hybrid vehicle a better buy than a conventional vehicle?

Hybrid cars are a good buy. They get excellent gas mileage without sacrificing size, interior space, speed, or acceleration. Most Americans are for anything that will lessen our dependence on foreign oil while also lessening our contribution to climate change. There are several hybrid cars available in the United States; Toyota Prius, Honda Civic Hybrid, Honda Insight,

Ford Fusion, Hyundai, and Buick La Crosse. There are certain to be more hybrid vehicles in the future.

Hybrid cars use both a small gasoline engine and an electric motor. The best known is the Toyota Prius, a parallel hybrid five-passenger aerodynamically slick (coefficient of drag is an extremely low .26) vehicle with a 1.5-liter gasoline engine and a 67-horsepower electric motor. It gets about 55 miles (89 kilometers) per gallon.

Parallel hybrid means that either the gas engine or the electric motor, or both, can drive the wheels. The Prius has a unique planetary gearset that receives power from the 1.5-liter gasoline engine or from the 67-horsepower electric motor. The planetary gearset can also send energy to a generator that charges batteries. The batteries then run the electric motor. The Toyota website has a nice streaming video of how the system works.

The Honda Civic Hybrid will go 650 miles (1,046 kilometers) between fill-ups. It has a four-cylinder, 1.3-liter, 85 horsepower gasoline engine. Honda claims 47 miles (75.6 kilometers) per gallon for their hybrid. Smaller engines are more efficient than big engines. When the engine is lighter, less energy is needed to accelerate the car. The pistons and other moving parts are smaller, requiring less energy every time they go up and down in the cylinders. The cylinders are smaller, also saving on gasoline.

Both the Toyota Prius and the Honda Civic Hybrid employ regenerative braking. Braking recharges the newer nickel-metal hydride (Ni-MH) batteries. In most of our cars, braking is done by friction between surfaces. The energy is lost as heat.

Hybrid cars help meet tough emissions standards. California has some of the tightest in the country. Hybrids help manufacturers meet the Corporate Average Fuel Economy (CAFE) standards. The present standards state that the average mileage of all new cars sold by a company must be 37.5 miles (60.5 kilometers per gallon for cars and 28.8 miles (46.3 kilometers) per gallon for trucks. If a car manufacturer sells one 60 miles per gallon hybrid, they can sell four gas-guzzling expensive cars that only get 20 miles (96.6 kilometers) per gallon. There's more profit in the gas guzzlers. Those auto manufacturing people are clever!

Hybrid vehicles are not new. Most train locomotives are diesel-electric. Giant mining trucks and some city buses also use diesel-electric. Submarines have been diesel-electric for 70 years or more, and newer subs are nuclear-electric. Now, you and I can also have a hybrid vehicle.

Although both Honda and Toyota are foreign manufacturers, they, like many so-called foreign carmakers, have plants here in the United States, employing American workers.

Along with hybrid vehicles, there are ever more all-electric vehicles coming out, such as the Tesla S, Honda Fit EV, Nissan Leaf, Toyota RAV4 EV, and Ford Focus Electric, to name just a few. Some of them are very powerful. A Tesla Model S can reach 155 miles (250 kilometers) per hour in 29 seconds.

Q70: *What do the lines in a Universal Product Code mean?*

The Universal Product Code (UPC), sometimes referred to as a bar code, is a product description code designed to be read by a computerized scanner at the cash register. The UPC permits fast checkout at the point of sale and gives the store owner an easy method to track sales and monitor inventory.

The UPC consists of 12 numbers in groups of zeroes (dark strips) and ones (white strips). The width of the strips matters. A bar is thin if it has only one strip and thicker if there are two or more strips set side by side. A big advantage of the UPC is that there are no letters or numbers, only the machine-scannable strip of black bars and white spaces.

The first number of a UPC is a description of the product. The next five numbers describe the product's manufacturer. The following five numbers describe the product itself, such as its size, weight, color, or some other distinguishing characteristic.

The last number is a check digit that is used to inform the scanner if there is an error in the other numbers. The preceding 11 digits, when added, multiplied, or subtracted in a certain way, will equal that 12th number. If they do not, a mistake has been made somewhere, perhaps because of a wrinkle or fold in the scanned label.

The price is never coded into the bars of the UPC. When the scanner at the checkout counter scans a package, the cash register sends the UPC number to the store's central point of sale computer to look up the UPC number. The central computer then sends back the actual price of the item. It happens almost instantly. The price is entered into the computer by the operator. That way, stores can decide at what price to sell an item, or the store can put the item on sale.

The end strips are "guard bars." There are also guard bars in the middle of the UPC. Numbers on the right side of the middle guard bars are optically the inverse of the numbers on the left. This inversion enables the bar code to be scanned from left-to-right or right-to-left. The scanning software knows if the code is the correct way or backward or upside down.

The first UPC item ever scanned was at Marsh's Supermarket in Troy, Ohio, on June 26, 1974. It was a 10-pack (50 sticks) of Wrigley's Juicy Fruit chewing gum, and the cash register rang up $0.67. That Juicy Fruit gum 10-pack is now on display at the Smithsonian National Museum of American History in Washington, DC.

UPC scanners use a very low wattage laser to read the product label. When supermarket scanners first came out in the middle 1970s, the word laser was omitted from any advertising. Lasers were associated with death rays, and who wants to go to the store to be zapped by a death ray? It does take time for us to accept some new technologies.

When the new nuclear magnetic resonance (NMR) machines appeared in hospitals a few decades ago, people were reluctant to use them because of the word *nuclear*. The medical profession changed the name to magnetic resonance imaging (MRI), and they became acceptable.

Q71: *How can we get more energy from the sun?*

We know we have dwindling supplies of fossil fuels: coal, oil, natural gas, and shale. That means we're in need of new ways of powering our planet. Fossil fuels are hydrocarbons formed from the remains of dead plants and animals. Even though some of these fossil fuels may last for a few hundred years, there is a finite supply.

Our nearest star, the sun, offers more than one solution to our energy needs. We're already harnessing the sun's energy to produce solar power. Photovoltaic cells (solar cells) directly convert light to electricity.

It may seem that solar energy is essentially free; however, creating the solar panels comes at a very high environmental cost. The mining of the materials and the manufacturing of the panels is costly. In addition, the output of solar panels is quite low compared to traditional means of generating electricity. Solar energy is here to stay and will remain an important slice of our energy needs, but it is not the complete solution.

Another idea is to use the energy of sunlight to create electricity that can break water down into its constituent parts of hydrogen and water, a process called electrolysis. The hydrogen can be used to provide clean energy for cars and trucks. It's the cleanest energy possible, no pollution. Unfortunately, the process is expensive.

Hydrogen-powered cars are being developed these days. The whole infrastructure of manufacturing, transporting the fuel, and fueling stations must be worked out. Safety considerations are primary. Like solar, hydrogen is here to stay and will remain an important segment of our energy needs. But it is not the complete solution.

Which leads us the ultimate use of the sun. There is ongoing research re-creating the process going on in the sun itself. Fusion is the activity that makes the sun shine. If we can harness that fusion, we just might solve the energy needs of mankind forever.

We are familiar with the process of fission. Fission is the splitting of atoms, usually uranium, that produces a tremendous amount of heat energy. Controlled fission is the process that goes on in a nuclear power plant. Uncontrolled reactions are atomic bombs. Not to fret, nuclear power plants do not have the proper fuel to explode.

Fusion is the process of squeezing together lighter atoms to make bigger atoms. Fusion is the reaction that goes on in the sun, where lighter hydrogen atoms are fused together to create heavier atoms of helium. A loss of mass occurs, and this loss is turned into pure energy in accordance with Einstein's famous equation $E = mc^2$. The total mass of the new atom is less than that mass of the two separate atoms. The missing mass is given off as energy.

Fusion occurs in an H bomb or hydrogen bomb. Tremendously high temperatures are required. Where do those high temperatures come from? An atomic bomb (A bomb) is detonated. In actual practice, the fusion material is packed around the atomic bomb.

The advantage of fusion over fission is that there is no nuclear waste to contend with. Whereas fission must be controlled and can "get away from you" as happened at Three Mile Island and Chernobyl, you must work very hard to get fusion to even occur. High temperatures and high pressures are required.

Thermonuclear fusion research has been going on since the 1950s. If harnessed, the payoff will be big, with practically no radiation, no waste, and no environmental pollution. The fuel is not uranium but simple water.

So far, scientists have not gotten more out of the fusion reaction compared to what they put in. When will fusion power be commercially feasible? Well, in about 20 years. But they have been saying "in about 20 years" for the last 60 years.

Fusion power will happen eventually. In the meantime, we rely on a mixture of fossil fuels, nuclear, solar, wind, hydroelectric, and biomass.

Chapter Eight

At the Fringes of Science

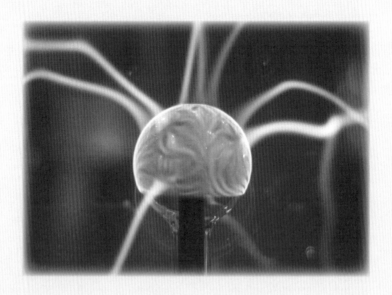

Q72: *Are there some trick questions in science?*

A student recently asked me a question that is often thought of as a trick question. It's one of those that "depends on" or has several possible interpretations or meanings. Let's look at a few of them.

If a tree falls in the forest and nobody is around, does it make a sound? The answer depends on your definition of sound. If sound is defined as motion of air caused by a vibrating body, then the tree makes a sound. If you think of sound as waves hitting a person's eardrum, then there is no sound because there is no ear to hear it.

When will we have the next full moon? Astronauts brought back more than 800 pounds (362.9 kilograms) of rock and soil samples from the moon between 1969 and 1972. The moon is partially depleted and will never be "full" again.

What color is a polar bear? A polar bear has white fur, but the skin underneath is dark or black. Each strand of the white fur acts as a fiber optic light pipe. The light is internally reflected through the hair strand to the skin of the bear. The skin absorbs all the solar energy it can get. The polar bear is black and white and warm all under!!

Q73: *How long would it take for someone to walk around the world?*

It is close to 25,000 miles (40,000 kilometers) (circumference) around the earth. The average walking speed for most people is about 3 miles (4.8 kilometers) per hour. We're looking at 8,300 hours of walking. Let's figure a 10-hour walking day. That puts us at 830 days of walking, or about 2.7 years.

Such a feat (no pun intended) would require about 50 million steps, many pairs of shoes, good health, determination, and stamina. It would be an epic demonstration of human endurance and courage.

But a walk around planet Earth is complicated. There is no path entirely on land that would permit a 25,000-mile continuous trek. One would have to take a boat or plane for a substantial part of the trip.

According to the *Guinness Book of World Records*, the first verified walk around the earth was made by Dave Kunst. It took four years, 21 million steps, and 22 pairs of leather shoes for Kunst to complete his record-making 14,450-mile walk in 1974. His brother John accompanied him, but he was killed by bandits in Afghanistan. Dave Kunst completed the journey with another brother, Pete. Kunst and his brothers hiked across Europe, North America, Asia, the Middle East, and back to Europe.

The *Guinness Book of World Records* lists Steve Newman as the first to walk around the world solo. It took Newman four years to cross 20 countries for a distance of 15,000 miles (24,000 kilometers).

Jean Béliveau, a neon sign salesman from Quebec, Canada, started his walk in 1998 at age 45. He hiked 45,000 miles (72,000 kilometers) through 64 countries in 11 years.

George Meegan holds the record for the longest unbroken walk. From 1977 to 1983, he walked 19,000 miles (31,000 kilometers) from Tierra Del Fuego, the southern tip of South America to the northernmost part of Alaska. Meegan covered the entire Western Hemisphere and the most degrees in latitude ever on foot.

There are ways of getting around the earth besides walking. Some notable circumnavigations include the Magellan-Elcano voyage. Magellan set out from Seville, Spain, in 1519 with five ships and 270 men. One ship, the *Victoria*, returned three years later with 18 men. Four ships were destroyed or lost, and Magellan himself was killed by hostiles in the Philippines.

The first airplane circumnavigation was carried out by the US Army Air Service in 1924. The team of fliers took 175 days to go 27,340 miles (44,000 kilometers). Four Douglas-built aircraft were used, and three finished the journey.

One of the most remarkable trips around the globe was the nine-day 1986 nonstop and non-refueled flight by Dick Rutan and Jeana Yeager. Their composite (fiberglass, carbon fiber, Kevlar) aircraft, Voyager, had 17 fuel tanks. Their Voyager aircraft can be seen at the Smithsonian National Air and Space Museum in Washington, DC.

Q74: Did an advanced technological civilization ever visit the earth?

According to polls reported by the *Huffington Post* and the National Geographic Society, nearly half of Americans believe UFOs or extraterrestrials have visited us, and 80 percent believe the government has concealed information about UFOs from the public.

It's little wonder, considering movies such as *Close Encounters of the Third Kind, Fire in the Sky, Men in Black, The X-Files* TV series, and numerous programs about Area 51, Roswell, and others. There must be something going on, the thinking goes.

But there exists no credible evidence of aliens, extraterrestrials, or UFOs having lived here or even having done a stopover. The fossil record has nothing to indicate that a technological species came before us.

It's useful to think about what we humans would leave behind if we all died out in the next few centuries. Let's say some advanced civilization folks visited in the next several hundred thousand years or even in a few million years.

Evidence of human habitation would be clear. Cities would be buried under plant life, roads all eroded away, and even steel towers corroded. But there would be plenty of evidence and clues to unearth, such as plastics, quarries, deposits of pure metal that had been mined and refined. Deep-penetrating radar would pick out those cities, buildings, millions of human-made structures, machines, art, tools, jet planes, rockets, microcircuits, nuclear reactors, and the written word.

Even if we all died out, our fossil remains could be found, analyzed, and dated. So if there had been any high-tech civilization before us, surely we would be able, by now, to find at least a couple, if not thousands, of artifacts they left behind. But as far as any science can determine, the earth was untouched by technology before humans came on the scene.

Some believers have pointed to the huge moai statues on Easter Island, the pyramids in Egypt, and the large geoglyph figures carved on the plains of Nazca in Peru, as proof of alien visitation and intervention. But we're continually amazed at the engineering feats of ancient peoples thousands of years ago. We should not be surprised at their accomplishments. After all, the brain in the skull of a human being 10,000 years ago is almost identical to the brain of modern man.

All the evidence of ETs is anecdotal and does not stand up to scientific scrutiny. Pictures of UFOs seem to be taken at night, are grainy, and lack detail. They are usually lights moving across the night sky. Discoveries at UFO crash sites are very suspect. There has been no verified interaction with aliens, dead or alive. Some things can't be explained, but that does not necessarily mean they are alien.

Any visit by extraterrestrials would involve travel from a distant solar system. It would take decades to make the trip from even a close neighbor such as Alpha Centauri, which is 4.2 light-years away—unless, of course, some really, really smart aliens have figured out a way to travel faster that the speed of light. But don't count on it. The speed of light, said Einstein, is the ultimate speed limit of the universe. Nothing can travel faster than the speed of light. It's been said that if you travel faster than the speed of light, God will pull you over.

Alien spacecraft are usually described as flying saucers. Alien beings are depicted as looking like us human beings. The portrayal of aliens and their craft are correlated closed with our biases and beliefs of what we think they should look like. We are seeing things as we want to see them and they fit our expectations.

Until evidence is presented and verified, the idea of alien visitations remains an enticing but unproven concept. So far, there's no proof that anyone has visited Earth from another planet. Still, it does raise the question: Is it even possible for a physical being to travel here and walk around unnoticed? Check your neighbors!

Q75: Will teleportation ever be possible?

Wouldn't that be nice? Just step into a transporter, say "Beam me up, Scotty," and you're instantly at school. Forget that long bus ride starting at 6:20 a.m. when it's still dark.

Teleportation is a mix of the words *telecommunication* and *transportation*. The process involves taking a physical object, like a human body, translating it into bits of data, sending the data somewhere, and putting it back together again.

There are trillions of atoms in the human body. Each of them would have to be disassembled, read, digitized, and transmitted, with the whole process reversed at the other end. Every atom would require a set of data on the type of atom, location, and energy state.

What about tolerance? If the person's repositioned molecules are even a hair's width off, the body would be a physiological and neurological mess. And what about all those neural connections in the brain that contain what we know as memory? Get those in disarray and it raises forgetfulness to a whole new plateau.

A bunch of British graduate students calculated the amount of time needed to transmit the necessary information for teleporting a human using the highest bandwidth available. Their answer put it at 350,000 times the age of the universe. No one knows how to collect and transmit that much information.

There is talk of a quantum computer, entangling particles, and processing information using individual atoms or particles instead of electronic integrated circuits. Such computers can outperform traditional computers, crack codes, and solve complex equations. They could lead to a quantum version of the Internet. The promise is great security and incredible privacy. Our government is reportedly working on such a computer.

One of the rules of quantum physics is known as the Heisenberg Uncertainty Principle. Heisenberg's principle says that you can know how fast something is moving or its location, but not both at the same time. Scientists have already gotten around the Heisenberg Uncertainty Principle by something called entanglement. They have coaxed photons (tiny packets of light) to tangle or interact, which means they share their traits. By using three photons, they can teleport one of them to a new place.

In July 2017, Chinese scientists successfully teleported an object from the earth's surface to an orbiting satellite for the first time ever. A photon, a tiny subatomic particle, was "transported" from the Gobi Desert to China's Micius satellite some 310 miles (498.9 kilometers) above the surface.

But don't get your hopes up. A single light particle is a far cry from a human body.

Q76: Is creating a real lightsaber possible?
. . . .

M ust be time for another Star Wars movie! Those lightsabers look so real and so very dangerous. And the sound effects that the producers put with the lightsaber makes it seem even more menacing. I looked at several websites that described these rod-like columns of glowing power.

Lightsabers are described in detail, but alas, they are not real. One website stated that a lightsaber is "like a sword on steroids." Any self-respecting lightsaber must be able to deflect and block the path of an opponent's lightsaber. Any of your top-of-the-line lightsabers can deflect blaster bolts and turn them back on the bad guy who fired them. Unfortunately, light cannot block light; in the real world, light beams pass through each other all the time.

I do love the language that is used. Words such as blade length adjusting knob, arc wave energy field, the Force, cycling field energizers, focusing crystal activator, power vortex ring, blade shroud emitter, energy modulation circuits, diatium power cell, and power field conductor. The use of scientific words and phrases is a well-known technique to make something that is fictional seem real.

Some websites do carry a warning disclaimer. Here is one of them: "Lightsabers are only a figment of George Lucas's imagination, of course. This is an entirely fictional article, based on information in Star Wars movies and books."

The Sharper Image store and website has the "official" Anakin Skywalker lightsaber with the "realistic, electroluminescent blue glow and ten motion-controlled, digitally recorded, signature Star Wars sound effects, including the authentic lightsaber and battle clash sounds that are activated on contact." It will set you back $120. Prefer the Darth Vader official lightsaber? Same cost as the Anakin Skywalker one, but with a red electroluminescent glow, instead of the blue.

Sadly, the closest we find to a lightsaber in real life are lasers that cut things like stone, leather, cloth, wood, metals, and plastics. They are widely used in industry. Lasers are well established in surgery. Laser eye surgery goes back 40 years. May the Force be with you!

Q77: What happens if you're driving at the speed of light and you turn on your headlights?

This is exactly the kind of question that Einstein asked himself at the age of 16. "What if I rode a beam of light across the universe? What would I see?" It took Einstein 10 years to find an answer. The short answer: "It can't be done."

Seems logical enough that I could get up to the speed of light. We all learned Newton's famous equation, $F = ma$. Apply a constant force (F) to a mass (m), and you get an acceleration (a), which means the object keeps going faster and faster, and it should get up to the speed of light and even beyond.

Yes, you could get close to the speed of light, but not light speed itself. As your car approaches the speed of light, its resistance or opposition to acceleration (mass) increases, so it would take an impossibly infinite force to actually reach the speed of light. The speed of light is given its own symbol (c).

Einstein's theory of special relativity shows that it is impossible to get to the speed of light. You cannot go at the speed of light, so the question is hypothetical. Only particles that have no mass (which is a contradiction) such as a photon of light can go at the speed of light.

If you did get close to the speed of light, you wouldn't notice anything different. Look in the mirror and you see yourself as if you were not moving. Unless you look out the side window, and watch the scenery passing you, you couldn't tell that you are moving at all. And how do you know that it is you that is moving? Perhaps your car is at rest and all that scenery is moving past you. All motion is relative.

Relativity seems counter-intuitive. If you are on a 100-mile-per-hour train and throw a fastball forward at 50 miles per hour, someone standing beside the track would measure the speed of the ball to be 100 miles per hour plus 50 miles per hour or 150 miles per hour. If you throw the ball 50 miles per hour toward the rear of the train, an observer beside the track would measure 100 miles per hour minus 50 miles per hour, or 50 miles per hour. Here are the metric equivalents: 100 miles = 160 kilometers; 50 miles = 80 kilometers.

But light does not work that way. Light travels at the same speed to all moving observers. Nothing different is observed for you moving at close to the speed of light, but it's a different story for people standing on the sidelines, so to speak. They would see your clocks running slow (time dilation). Your car would be compressed along your direction of motion (length contraction). Mass would increase. There is an equation that can be used to calculate these relativistic effects.

It's grand to think about time, space, and matter. But the laws of the universe have a way of grounding us in reality. Asking what we would see if we're traveling at the speed of light is tantamount to asking such questions as "Could I build a perpetual motion machine?" or "Can I divide by zero?" There are no answers to these questions. The questions themselves are flawed.

Q78: Why do people say our *"fate is in the stars"*?

∙ ∙

The question refers to astrology. The dictionary defines astrology as the study of the movement and relative position of celestial objects as a means for divining information about human affairs and terrestrial events.

Here is what one website advertisement for horoscope readings says about astrology:

> *A horoscope allows one to know or make predictions about the future. It is based on planetary positions to guide the humans, as their behavior is influenced from stellar bodies and their phases. It provides essential tips on likely events so that individuals can decide future courses of action. These predictions using horoscope are made by astrologers and the science is astrology. The use of horoscopes in predictions dates to at least five thousand years ago. Any individual can use horoscope predictions for a better future and safe ventures in family or business.*

The basis of astrology is simple: A person's character and destiny can supposedly be understood from the positions of the sun, moon, and planets at the moment of his or her birth. Interpreting the location of these bodies using a chart called the horoscope, astrologers claim to predict and explain the course of life and help people make decisions. Astrologers believe that the important constellations are the ones the sun passes through during the course of a year. These are the constellations of the zodiac.

Note: Do not confuse astrology with astronomy. Astronomy is a legitimate science, the science that studies celestial objects and phenomena. It applies mathematics, physics, and chemistry in an effort to explain the origin of those objects and phenomena and their evolution.

Simply put: Astrology doesn't work. Horoscopes are pure hogwash. Many careful tests have shown that, despite their claims, astrologers really can't predict anything. A French statistician Michel Gauquelin sent the horoscope for one of the worst mass murderers in French history to 150 people and asked how well it fit them. 94 percent of the subjects said they recognized themselves in the description.

Researcher Geoffrey Dean reversed the astrological readings of 22 subjects, substituting phrases that were the opposite of what the horoscopes actually stated. Yet the subjects in this study said the readings applied to them just as often (95 percent of the time) as people to whom the correct phrases were given. No wonder that astrological predictions are written in the vaguest and most general language possible.

Along with astrologers, there are psychics and tarot card readers willing to part us from our money. We should not be tied to an ancient fantasy, left over from a time when humans huddled by the campfire, afraid of the night.

Have fun by reading your horoscope in the daily newspaper, but don't place any stock in it. Do you notice that the horoscope is most often placed on the same page as the comics? Remember that line from Shakespeare's *Julius Caesar*, spoken by Cassius: "Men at some time are masters of their fates. The fault, dear Brutus, is not in our stars, but in ourselves."

Horoscopes belong in the same category as other frauds such as Bigfoot, aliens among us, perpetual motion machines, cold fusion, water witching, crop circles, and a second shooter on the grassy knoll, to name a few. My horoscope this morning says that I may encounter some pushback on my list of frauds.

Q79: Could we drill a hole all the way through the earth?

In theory, one could drill a hole through the earth, but it would be extremely difficult in practice. The deepest hole ever drilled for research purposes was the Kola Superdeep Borehole, on the Kola Peninsula in the former Soviet Union, east of Norway. The Soviet drillers found hydrogen gas and water trapped in the rocks. The drillers got down to a tad more than 40,000 feet (12,000 meters), which is 7.8 miles (12.2 kilometers). Considering that the earth is 8,000 miles (12,875 kilometers) in diameter, they did not get very much of the way. After the fall of the Soviet Union, the project was abandoned.

The Soviet attempt was expensive. Workers drilled for 19 years, with many drill bits, broken shafts, and secondary holes. They only made it through one third of the crust. The drill bits encountered intense heat (356°F/180°C) at 7 miles (11.3 kilometers) down. If they had reached their target of 49,000 feet (15,000 meters), the calculated temperature of 570°F (299°C) degrees would have made the drill bits useless.

The Kola Superdeep Borehole, meant for research, has since been surpassed by two oil wells. The first is 40,318-foot (12,289-meter) oil well dug in Qatar in 2008, and the second a 40,502-foot (12,345-meter) offshore oil well dug in 2011 near the Russian island of Sakhalin off the Russian eastern coast, not far from Japan. The borehole for the Russian well is 9 inches (23 centimeters) in diameter.

The earth is made up of the crust, which is 3 to 30 miles (5 to 48 kilometers) thick—3 miles under the ocean and 30 miles on the continents. The crust makes up about one percent of the volume of the earth.

Then comes the solid hot shell called the mantle, which is 1,800 miles (2,900 kilometers) thick. The mantle makes up about 85 percent of the earth's volume.

The core, made of nickel and iron, has two layers, a liquid outer layer and an inner solid layer. The core makes up about 15 percent of our planet.

Why drill a hole in the earth when we already know what's there? Using seismographs and computer simulations, scientists have developed theories about the internal structure of the earth. The manner in which seismic waves reflect off the interior of the earth gives scientists many clues as to the internal structure. It may not be necessary to drill through the earth to build up a fairly detailed understanding of what is below our feet.

If you did manage to dig a hole all the way through the earth, and jumped in, what would happen?

If there was no friction, including air resistance, it would take about 42 minutes to reach the other end of the tunnel. At first, the pull of gravity would make you go faster and faster. Reaching the center of the earth in about 21 minutes, you would be going about 18,000 miles (29,000 kilometers) per hour. But then, as you passed the center, gravity would slow you down.

After another 21 minutes, with gravity slowing you as you go, you would reach the far side and stop briefly in midair. Unless someone caught you, you'd then head back the way you came and start all over again. In our idealized case, this would continue indefinitely, like a pendulum or a spring, in a process called simple harmonic motion.

If there is any kind of resistance, such as touching the side of the tunnel, or air in the tunnel, some energy is lost. You wouldn't quite reach the other end and would go zinging back down into the tunnel. Your yo-yoing back and forth would finally leave you stuck in the middle, with a long, hot climb home. It's much like being in a swing. Push off once, and you go back and forth, but the swing finally stops swinging.

When I was a boy on the Seneca, Wisconsin farm on Oak Grove Ridge, my brothers and I discussed digging a hole through the earth. It came up numerous times as we dug holes for fencing posts. Dad would say "dig a little deeper," to which one of us would respond "if I dig any deeper, the hole will come out in China." Little did we realize that China is entirely in the northern hemisphere. If we had dug deep enough, we would have come out somewhere in the Indian Ocean, not China.

Chapter Nine

Science Mystery and History

Q80: *What are germs?*

I t's hard to believe that something we can't even see can make us very sick and even kill us. We are so big and these creatures are so tiny. It just doesn't seem like a fair fight. Yet, microscopic organisms sometimes win.

There are four major categories of germs: bacteria, viruses, fungi, and protozoa. The ones most likely to harm us are bacteria and viruses.

Bacteria are one-celled organisms that get their nourishment from their environment, which in many cases is our body. Bacteria can live inside or outside the body. Bacteria can cause infections, such as sore throat, pneumonia, ear aches, and tooth cavities. The dreaded bubonic plague, or Black Death, was caused by bacteria. In the fourteenth century, the Black Death killed an estimated 25 million people, a quarter to a third of the European population.

The Oregon Trail is strewn with the graves of those who died of typhoid fever, cholera, and dysentery. All of these illnesses were caused by bacteria that thrived in poor sanitary conditions and contaminated water. It is estimated that 10 people died for every mile on the trail, the vast majority due to cholera. A young husky pioneer might hitch up the team of horses or oxen in the morning, start walking with his family along with others in the wagon train, and be dead by sunset. The cholera bacteria sucked water from the body into the intestines, leading to continual discharge, resulting in severe and often fatal dehydration.

If you want to read a really good medical detective story, look up John Snow. In 1854, Dr. Snow made a map of cholera cases in London and pinpointed the source of the outbreak to a public well on Broad Street that had been dug only 3 feet (0.9 meters) from an old cesspool. It was the first time in which statistical analysis led to an effective approach to preventing serious infections. Removing the handle of the pump so people could no longer get to the contaminated water saved the life of a great many people.

Most bacteria can be killed by boiling water or adding chlorine or disinfectants. When people develop serious infections due to bacteria, they can often be cured with antibiotics such as penicillin.

Not all bacteria are bad. Good bacteria in our intestines help digest food. Bacteria in laboratories help scientists produce medicines and vaccines.

Viruses are a hundred times smaller than bacteria and were first seen by the electron microscope in 1931. Viruses don't last for long unless they are inside a host, and they must be inside our body cells to reproduce. Viruses cannot divide by themselves. Instead, the virus invades the host cell and takes over some of the manufacturing machinery inside the cell. As a result, the virus forces the cell to produce thousands of copies of the original virus.

Viruses reproduce rapidly because they only have a few genes, compared to humans who have 20,000 to 25,000 genes. They cause colds, flu, measles, chickenpox, HIV/AIDS, and hepatitis, to name a few.

Viruses are sneaky. Some are latent, lying dormant and inactive for many years before causing illness; the virus that causes the painful condition called shingles is an example of this.

Infections that are due to viruses can't be treated with antibiotics, but many viral infections can be prevented with appropriate immunizations. There is now even a shingles vaccine, recommended for people who are older than age 50.

Viruses can be spread through the air by coughs and sneezes. Contamination of food and water, transmission of body fluids from person to person, and bites from bloodsucking insects are ways that different viruses can be spread.

Because viruses contain genes, they can mutate and evolve. That's why there is no cure for the common cold. If medical science finds a "cure for the cold," the wily virus will merely change, or mutate, and render the "cure" ineffective.

Bacteria of course contain genes, too. They also can mutate and evolve. In fact, they can share genes with other bacteria and increase their ability to resist antibiotics.

One virus that recently caused tons of concern and fear is Ebola. It's a relatively new virus, discovered in 1976 by a microbiology student in Belgium who got a blood sample from a Belgian nun who had died in Zaire. A large outbreak of Ebola in West Africa in 2014 killed more than 11,000 people. Another recent scare was caused by the Zika virus, which is spread by mosquitoes. Pregnant women who come down with Zika may give birth to babies with a birth defect known as microcephaly—an abnormally small brain.

Immunization is essential to help prevent the spread of diseases due to "germs," including some diseases due to viruses that antibiotics can't treat, like the viruses that cause measles, mumps, rubella, influenza, and hepatitis B. Immunization can also prevent severe reactions to bacterial toxins that would otherwise be fatal. This occurs, for example, with tetanus and anthrax. The Centers for Disease Control and Prevention has a website that explains which vaccines are appropriate for people of different ages.

Q81: Why is the right side of a ship called starboard and the left side called port?

Viking ships were maneuvered with a long board on the right side near the back. The word *starboard* is derived from *steor* for "steering" and *bord* for "board." This steering board was the rudder that controlled the direction of the ship. Thus, the right side became known as the starboard side.

The Viking longboats were loaded from the left side to prevent damage to the steering paddle located on the right or starboard side. *Lade* or *lar* means "load" and *bord* means "side." Hence the name became *larboard* or left side.

But the name starboard and larboard sound much alike and could cause confusion when shouting orders over the wind, weather, and waves. The British Admiralty demanded that the word *port* be used in place of larboard. It does make sense, because the boat is loaded while in port and via the port side. The US Navy officially adopted the term *port* in 1846.

Ships and seafaring have greatly enriched our language. A butt is a wooden cask holding water and to scuttle means to drill a hole or tap a cask. The sailors of old would exchange gossip when they gathered around the scuttlebutt for a drink of water.

The French phrase *m'aidez* means "help me." This "mayday" call is now the distress call for vessels and people in trouble at sea and in the air. It was made official by the International Telecommunications Conference in 1948.

A clean bill of health was an official document given to a ship that had left a port in which there was no epidemic or infectious diseases occurring.

Wooden ships had decks made of planks. The space between planks was filled with a packing material called oakum, a tarred fiber used for caulking the joints. The joints were sealed with a mixture of pitch and tar. These blackened joints left a visible series of lines running the length of the ship and were spaced 6 to 8 inches (15 to 20 centimeters) apart.

Most every Sunday, a warship's crew was ordered to fall in or line up in formation at a designated area based on every crewmember's job. In order to have a neat alignment, sailors were directed to stand with their toes just touching a particular seam.

These seams were also used for punishment. The captain might order a naughty young sailor or cabin boy to stand with his toes just touching a designated seam for hours at a time, and not talk to anyone. Older sailors were flogged. Obviously, this "toe the line" was an admonishment to a miscreant that it just might be less painful and more pleasant to conduct himself in the required manner.

Q82: Why does the frost line extend deeper even as the air gets warmer in spring?

I f you want to know how deep the frost is, just ask the guys who dig graves, or the fellows who work on city water and sewer systems, or those who put in basements in new construction, or electric line workers. The frost we're talking about is not that sparkling white stuff you see on lawns, windshields, and rooftops. We are referring to water in the ground or soil that has frozen and is as solid as ice. Well, it really is ice! As the air gets cold, the ground also gets extremely cold, and the water in the soil freezes. The "frost line," or the maximum depth to which this frozen soil extends, grows greater and greater throughout the winter. In the 48 contiguous United States, the frost line never goes lower than about 8 feet (2.4 meters). Below that, the soil temperature is always above freezing.

The downward advance of frozen ground might be 1 inch (2.5 centimeters) per day, at best. How deep and how fast depends on time, temperature, and insulation. The insulation is snow cover. Snow is very good at insulating the ground. Lots of snow, especially early in the winter, and the frost line does not go down very far, maybe only a few inches.

The advance of the frost line downward is caused by the freezing of the ground below the frozen part. Water next to frozen water (ice) will freeze, regardless of the air temperature above.

So even as air temperature starts to warm in the spring, the frost will go deeper and deeper until the now thawing ground catches up. In a way this seems to defy logic. As one author wrote in an article I read: "The frost will go deeper despite the surface temperature, not because of it."

In some northern places in Alaska and Canada, the top layer of soil thaws come spring and summer. However, during the short summer season, the "thaw line" will go down but never get to the bottom of the frozen soil. There remains a layer of perpetually frozen ground, hence the name permafrost.

Because the top layer of soil above the permafrost is unfrozen, it supports grasses, scrubs, flowers, and small bushes; the tundra is green with vegetation in the Arctic summer. But you won't find any large trees, such as oaks, elms, and maples, because the unfrozen ground does not go deep enough to support tree roots.

The thickest ice ever recorded is almost 3 miles (5 kilometers), but that was over the Antarctic landmass. The thickest lake ice is reported to be Lake Vostok, also in Antarctica. In 2012, a team of scientists bored an ice core of 12,400 feet (3,780 meters) before hitting lake water. No report on any fish caught!

Q83: How did Eratosthenes measure the size of the earth?

Phillip V, king of Macedonia, commissioned Eratosthenes to measure the circumference of the earth in the year 240 BCE. Today the countries of Croatia, Bosnia, Herzegovina, Montenegro, and Serbia sit where Macedonia was. It was already known that the earth was a sphere, but no one knew how big a sphere.

Eratosthenes was a librarian in the city of Alexandria, where the Nile River flows into the Mediterranean Sea. Alexandria had the most famous library in the known world. Eratosthenes had read that at noon on the summer solstice (June 21) in the city of Syene, Egypt, a vertical rod did not cast a shadow, but at his house in Alexandria, some 5,000 *stadia* (500 miles/800 kilometers) north, on the very same day and time, a vertical rod cast a shadow of a bit more than 7 degrees.

There's another account that Eratosthenes read that on June 21, no shadow was cast in a well at Syene at high noon. Same idea, well or rod, it doesn't make any difference.

Eratosthenes set up a simple ratio of 7 degrees divided by 360 degrees equals 500 miles (800 kilometers) divided by the unknown circumference. This yielded a circumference for the earth of 25,710 miles (41,380 kilometers). That comes mighty close to the true circumference of almost 25,000 miles (40,000 kilometers).

Eratosthenes was a mathematics and science genius. He devised a system of latitude and longitude and a calendar that included leap years. He compiled a star catalog that showed 675 stars. Eratosthenes invented a mechanical device used by early astronomers to demonstrate and predict the apparent motions of the stars in the sky.

Some researchers claim that Eratosthenes measured the distance from the earth to the moon and the distance from the earth to the sun. Any proof of those accomplishments has been lost.

Eratosthenes yearned to understand the complexities of the entire world. In his three-volume work *Geography*, he described and mapped his entire known world, dividing the earth into five climate zones: two freezing zones around the poles, two temperate zones, and a zone encompassing the equator and the tropics. We continue to use the system today. Eratosthenes is considered the Father of Geography and has a crater on the moon named after him.

In old age, Eratosthenes became blind and died of self-induced starvation. He lived to age 82, quite remarkable for that time period.

Q84: Is it true that the universe is running down?

The process of running down and becoming disordered is an inescapable law of physics. Metal rusts, foods rot, flowers wither, ice cubes melt, eggs break, and we age. The process is often referred to as "the arrow of time." The direction of the arrow of time is from order to disorder.

Imagine an eye dropper of food dye poised above a glass of water. A slight squeeze on the bulb and the dye drops into the water and diffuses throughout the water. Order to disorder. You won't expect the dye to come together and concentrate again in the eyedropper. Break an egg onto a skillet. Again, there is that order to disorder. Don't expect the egg to come back together again.

Leave a flashlight on, and eventually the bulb gets dimmer and dimmer until it finally goes out. The electricity-generating chemicals get mixed up in the battery and become disordered.

The energy of gasoline is organized and useful energy. The gas burns in the engine. Part of the energy does work in moving the pistons, part heats the engine, and part of the energy goes out the exhaust. Useful energy degenerates to non-useful forms and is not available for doing the same work again, such as driving another car. It's that order to disorder.

Energy in the form of electricity goes into lighting our homes and degenerates into heat energy.

This idea of "running down" is tied into the laws of thermodynamics. The first law says that energy cannot be created or destroyed, only changed to another form. The second law states that heat flows from hot to cold. Entropy is a measure of the amount of disorder. Nature tends to disorder, and disorder and entropy are always increasing. There are formulas that quantify the amount of disorder or entropy.

So, yes, the universe is running down. But there is a long way to go and it should be at the bottom of our list of worries.

There are some cases where the reverse is true, small islands where living things take in energy and use it to create order and beauty. The six-sided wax combs inside a beehive show how living things can organize matter. The honeycomb is built with mathematical accuracy to give maximum strength and storage space with a minimum use of materials. The bees are guided entirely by instinct.

The exquisite pattern of a spiderweb or cobweb is created by the spider taking in energy to create order from disorder, from seemingly nothing to something structurally superb. The tensile strength of the spider material is greater than the same weight of steel and has much greater elasticity. Researchers are looking at spider web material for potential use in bullet-proof vests and artificial tendons.

All through the natural world we see examples where living things make order out of disorder. The seashell, the peacock feather, and plant cell structure are all such examples. All require some form of energy input. The energy of raw materials, water, and sunlight, are taken in by life-forms to create order from disorder, order from chaos.

Q85: Why are polls sometimes wrong?
· ·

Political polls nationwide are remarkably accurate. You will notice that they always say something like, "This poll has an accuracy of plus or minus 3 to 5 percent." The secret, and it really is not a secret, is that the sample must be representative of the population being surveyed. The size of the sample is not that important. What is important is that the sample truly reflects the general public being canvassed.

Marketing firms that mainly use the Internet or magazine surveys are notoriously inaccurate. The questions are framed to elicit the response wanted. Pay particular attention to who is paying for any survey or poll. Politicians most often want honest answers, but sometimes they fish for responses they can plant as news items.

The telephone has long been the pollster's main tool, as we all learn when the political season rolls around. But more Americans are refusing to play the game. With caller ID, some people choose not to pick up the phone. More people, pollsters say, are apathetic to politics and choose not to respond. Many younger potential voters no longer have land lines and use only cell phones. Identifying the people from whom to draw a representative sample is getting more problematic.

Pollsters, whether for politics, sports, or products, are shifting a bit in their approach. For example, voters are sometimes asked, "Who do you think will win?" rather than, "Who will you vote for?" Companies call these techniques "prediction markets."

Before 2016, there were two notable national poll blunders. The 1936 election was between President Franklin D. Roosevelt and the Republican challenger Alfred Landon. A popular magazine, *Literary Digest*, sent out 10 million postcards in 1936 to try to predict the winner of the Roosevelt-Landon race. One quarter of those, 2.5 million, were returned. The results indicated a big 57 percent to 43 percent win for Alf Landon. Meanwhile, another up-and-coming pollster, George Gallup, confidently predicted just the opposite, with a 56 percent win for Roosevelt.

What went wrong? *Literary Digest* sent out those 10 million cards by scouring a list of people who owned telephones and cars. In 1936, only the well-to-do and upper middle class had telephones and cars.

George Gallup polled only 50,000 people, which is .005, or half of one percent of what the *Literary Digest* did. But Gallup used a representative sample. He made sure that his 50,000 were a good cross-section of the American electorate.

Gallup earned the title of most trusted pollster in American and the *Literary Digest*'s reputation was in ruins. *Literary Digest* polls did not have a representative sample, but Gallup did.

The 1948 election between President Harry Truman and Republican opponent Thomas Dewey was another shining example of polls gone wrong. The three main polling organizations at the time, Gallup, Roper, and Crossley, all predicted a Dewey win of about 5 or 6 percent. The *Chicago Tribune* was so confident of a Dewey win, it printed that famed headline "Dewey Defeats Truman." In fact, just the opposite happened. Truman won by five percentage points, 50–45. What went wrong?

All three polling companies used "quota sampling." Each hired interviewer was assigned a set number of voters in various categories, such as sex, age, race, economic status, and site of residence. The obvious intent was to get a sample representation of the population in every essential respect.

The companies did not specify how the data was gathered, such as personal interviews, mailings, head counts at church meetings, etc. What a good many of these hired people did was to telephone voters and ask them who they planned to vote for. Even in 1948, lots of poorer folks did not have telephones, especially in rural areas. At that time, Republicans were easier to get a hold of and interview than Democrats. The samples of all three pollsters were not representative of the voting population.

The 2016 presidential election was certainly interesting. Most every polling entity predicted a Clinton victory, although the results were within the margin of error.

Q86: Is there any evidence humans are still evolving?
. . . .

No topic is more controversial in religious circles than the evolution of man. The word *evolution* is scary to some folks because it conjures up images of "humans coming from the apes or monkeys." A better word to use would be *change*. And yes, everything is in a state of change: humans, the earth, our environment, the universe.

All life changes over time to become as well suited as possible for whatever environment it finds itself in. Life seeks to attain a comfortable environment or niche that no other species is using, so competition for resources is lessened, and to get to that state using the least possible amount of effort or energy.

Humans are changing so rapidly that some physical trait variations can be seen in only a few thousand years. Let's look at some examples.

About one third of modern humans do not develop wisdom teeth. Around 100,000 years ago, humans had big jaws that required powerful molar teeth in the back to grind up plants for digestion. These days we cut up our plants, for example by grinding wheat into flour. There is no longer any advantage to having those wisdom teeth. People born without wisdom teeth suffer no adaptive disadvantage. They do not need to go through the fuss and pain, and staying home from school and missing work to have wisdom teeth removed. For many people, wisdom teeth are no longer trying to crowd into a jaw that is now too short to hold them.

We tend to forget these evolutionary changes take a long time. It's estimated that in another 100,000 years a majority of people will no longer grow wisdom teeth. For that to happen, people without wisdom teeth need to survive better and have more children than people who do have wisdom teeth.

There is some speculation that in the future, we may no longer require a super-strength immune system. We've conquered many deadly diseases, such as smallpox and bubonic plagues that decimated populations in the past. The chances of contracting these diseases today is extremely low. In the future, we may have no need for an immune system that can respond rapidly to a smallpox infection.

Does having a strong immune system able to respond to vanishing diseases carry any cost? It's possible that an overly responsive immune system might be more likely to come down with autoimmune diseases like lupus or rheumatoid arthritis. These very reactive people might be more likely to suffer from asthma. If any of these disorders make a person likely to have fewer children, we could evolve toward less active immunity—but it will take hundreds of generations.

Lactose intolerance is the inability to digest lactose (milk sugar) using an enzyme called lactase. Babies can digest lactose; they have the lactase enzyme. Most people's bodies stop making the lactase enzyme as we get older. Around 10,000 years ago, Europeans started producing lactase all the way into adulthood. Those people with the lactase enzyme were more successful, because they could get protein and calories from herding. They produced more children, so the trait was passed down. The change is believed to be the result of several genetic mutations occurring over time. The trait for lactose tolerance, the ability to drink milk without encountering symptoms, is now in 35 percent of the population. It occurs in sections of the population whose ancestors raised lots of milk-producing animals.

Charles Darwin, in his book *On the Origin of Species*, never addressed the question of human evolution. He only argued for the idea of new species evolving from earlier ones. He left human development for future researchers. He stated, "Light will be thrown on the origin of man and his history."

Yes, we are changing, evolving, and adapting to our ever-changing environment. These changes are so slow and gradual that we never notice them in a lifetime or even over several generations.

Wouldn't it be great if we could be evolving spiritually, morally, and ethically, leading to an end to the scourge of war and a balanced distribution of the bounty of the Earth's riches? That would be an evolutionary change that all humans would celebrate.

Q87: What is the world's oldest shipwreck?

That would be the Bronze Age ship, *Uluburun*, accidentally found by a Turkish sponge diver in 1982. The young sponge diver told his captain that he had seen strange "metal biscuits with ears" lying on the ocean floor. The divers were in the eastern Mediterranean Sea, off the southern coast of Turkey, near Kas, working at a depth of 150 feet (45.7 meters).

The captain recognized this description as that of a Bronze Age copper ingot. Archaeologists explored the site for 10 years beginning in 1984. Divers made more than 22,000 dives. Because of the extreme depth, dive time was limited to 20 minutes each and two dives per day.

Archaeologists dated the ship to 1300 BCE. They found items representing the seven civilizations that flourished in the eastern Mediterranean at the time of the reign of Tutankhamun in Egypt and the fall of Troy. The timbers of the 50-foot (15-meter) vessel were fastened together with mortise-and-tenon joints pinned with hardwood pegs, just the way Homer described the construction of the ship of Odysseus. The ship had a single mast, a prow both forward and aft, and one large steering oar off to one side that served as the rudder.

The main cargo was 10 tons (9 metric tons) of copper ingots, along with tin ingots (which were used with copper to make bronze), a golden chalice, and some of the earliest known pieces of glass. The oxhide ingot shape (those strange "biscuits with ears") had four legs or handles for easy lifting and transportation on horseback. Other products included ebony logs from Egypt that matched the ebony found in the furniture in King Tut's tomb. Fishing gear, pottery, amber beads, resins, mollusk shells, hippopotamus teeth, tortoise shells, ostrich eggshells, weaponry, tools, and jewelry were discovered.

The resin was used in incense. The tortoiseshells were used as sound boxes in musical instruments, such as the lute. Ostrich eggshells became containers. Hippopotamus teeth were used to create ivory inlays.

Foodstuffs found with the vessel included nuts, figs, olives, grapes, spices, and grain. A small wooden "book" with ivory hinges, probably representing the world's oldest known book, was found. The wooden pages of the book had been spread with a wax, which would have been inscribed with a pen or stylus.

A gold scarab (medallion) bearing the royal seal of Queen Nefertiti of Egypt was brought up. It is the only one known in existence. Nefertiti was the wife of Egyptian pharaoh Akhenaten who ruled for 17 years.

The contents of the *Uluburun* suggested the cargo was meant for royalty. The sinking may have been a severe blow to important persons in the 14 century BCE. But it was a serendipitous discovery that provided an enormous amount of new information about that ancient era.

An article in *National Geographic* points out that sponge divers provide the best information about ancient shipwrecks. "Far more valuable than the most sophisticated sonar or magnetometers," states shipwreck explorer George Bass.

In a typical summer, 25 boats are working off the coasts of Turkey and Greece looking for sponges. An old shipwreck is a lucky find.

Chapter Ten

Chemistry and the Atom

Q88: Why is lead dangerous to humans?

L ead is toxic to everyone, but especially to unborn babies and young children. Lead is a dangerous poison that can be absorbed through the skin, inhaled, or swallowed. It can be absorbed more readily by bodies that are developing and growing than by adults whose bodies are fully mature.

Lead poisoning causes a wide range of medical problems, including stomach pains, hearing problems, posture difficulties, headaches, decreased intelligence, attention deficit, learning problems, anemia, and behavioral issues. It has severe effects on a child's developing brain.

What makes lead so dangerous? Once it gets inside a person's system, it is distributed throughout the body, just like the helpful minerals that you need, such as calcium, iron, zinc, potassium, and phosphorus. In the bloodstream, lead damages red blood cells. Red blood cells carry oxygen to the body. Damage to red blood cells make a person anemic, and anemic people are tired all the time. Most of the lead ends up in the bones, and bones absorb calcium. Calcium is needed for strong bones and good teeth, as well as muscle contraction and nerve function. Absorbed lead (which you don't want) displaces the calcium (which you do want). One of the menacing features of lead toxicity is that lead can reside in a person's body for decades. No threshold for lead exposure has been found. That is another way of saying that any amount of lead can be harmful.

Where does lead come from? Lead is found naturally in the earth. Lead poisoning has historically been caused by lead-lined water pipes, gasoline, and paint. Fortunately, lead pipes once used to carry drinking water are now banned. Leaded gasoline was banned in the 1970s. Leaded paint has been a big problem. Little kids sometimes gnaw on painted windowsills and furniture and ingest the paint chips. Although leaded paint was outlawed in the 1970s, it remains in some older homes. Today, toys from overseas continue to be an issue. Millions of toys from China were recalled in 2007 because of lead paint.

In 2014, the city of Flint, Michigan, switched its water supply from Lake Huron to the notorious Flint River. The idea was to save money. Soon after the switch, the water started to look brown, taste bad, and smell funny. The brown color came from the iron. The water was not treated and the highly corrosive water damaged the water pipes. That was not the worst of it. About half the service pipes in Flint were made of lead. Lead started leaching into the water supply. Corrective action has now been taken.

Wisconsin has a rich tradition of lead mining. In the 1830s, experienced miners from Cornwall, England, built their limestone houses in Grant, Iowa, and Lafayette counties. By 1840, more than 4,000 miners were mining lead around Mineral Point and New Diggings in the southwest corner of the state. They dug into the hillside like the furry animal named the badger. That's why Wisconsin is known as the Badger State. Most of the lead ammunition for Union troops in the Civil War came from Wisconsin.

An obvious question is: "Why don't we get rid of all lead and stop mining the stuff?" Answer: Lead is valuable and necessary. Lead is used in our car batteries, the lead-acid storage kind. Lead is also used in fishing lures, ballast for sailing boats, ammunition, radiation shielding in medical and dental facilities, and glassware. We need lead, but we must continue to find ways to prevent it from getting into our bodies.

Q89: What is vulcanization?

Columbus and his Spanish buddies found natives on Hispaniola (now Haiti and the Dominican Republic) playing games with a ball formed from the discharge of a tree. The

Spanish explorers brought some of this "India gum" back to Europe, but at first, no good use could be found for it. Then Joseph Priestley, English theologian and chemist, and the discoverer of oxygen, showed that the gum could *rub* out pencil marks. Thus, it received its present name, *rubber*, from this useful, somewhat trivial application.

No important use for rubber was found for more than 200 years. Natural rubber became soft and sticky at high temperatures and stiff and brittle at low temperatures. Then a Scottish fellow by the name of Charles Macintosh pressed two pieces of cloth together with a layer of rubber between them. He developed a waterproof coat. The name mackintosh is still used in England for rainwear. Both England and the United States made boots and shoes using rubber, but the results were not favorable: stiff in winter, soft and shapeless in summer.

Charles Goodyear was born in New Haven, Connecticut, in 1800. He was determined to make rubber useful by making it resistant to temperature changes. His path to discovery was a long and arduous journey, taking a toll on his health and wealth. At one point, he was in debtor's prison, dependent on friends and relatives for food and housing. He sold the government a large order of mailbags impregnated with rubber to make them waterproof, but they turned shapeless and sticky from the heat before they left the factory.

One day, Goodyear accidentally allowed a mixture of rubber and sulfur to touch a hot stove. Instead of melting, the rubber only charred slightly as a piece of leather would. Goodyear nailed the slab of gum-like material outside the kitchen door in the intense cold. In the morning, he brought it in, holding it up exultingly. He found it to be as flexible as it was when he put it out. In the following months, Goodyear determined the optimum temperature and time of heating for stabilizing the rubber-sulfur mix. He applied for and was issued a patent in 1844. The process of mixing sulfur to rubber he termed vulcanization, after the Roman god of fire, Vulcan.

When natural rubber is heated with sulfur, the sulfur atoms link the long chain molecules of rubber, stabilizing them and making the rubber matrix much less sensitive to temperature changes. The sulfur atoms make cross-links and bridges, creating a mesh-like material that no longer allows the long chains of rubber molecules to move independently of each other.

Vulcanization of rubber led to a multitude of useful applications; boots, shoes, tires, hoses, conveyor belts, gaskets for seals, and even hockey pucks. By 1858, the value of rubber goods sold reached more than $5 million. The Goodyear Company was founded in Akron, Ohio, a few decades later.

As often happens in these invention cases, Charles Goodyear was not a lived-happily-ever-after kind of guy. He became embroiled in defending his patent and never recovered from his huge and mounting debts. The many lawsuits and years of working with harsh chemicals took a toll on Charles Goodyear. He died on his way to see his own dying daughter on July 1, 1860 at age 59.

Goodyear and his wife, Clarissa, raised four daughters and one son. The son, Charles Goodyear Jr. invented a shoemaking technique, called the Goodyear welt. In 1869, he invented the machinery needed to stitch the outsole to the insole by using the Howe sewing machine.

Q90: How can you tell an acid from a base?

T he measure of the activity of the hydrogen ions in a solution is termed the pH of that solution. The letter *p* stands for potential, and the letter *H* is for hydrogen. The pH of pure water is about seven and is considered neutral. Solutions less than seven are acidic, and a reading higher than seven is basic or alkaline.

There are several indicators that will test the pH of a substance. The simplest is based on a strip of paper changing color. Litmus paper will turn red if put in an acid and blue-green if dipped in a base. There are several other indicators commercially available, such as thymol blue, methyl red, and phenolphthalein.

You can make your own indicator by putting a few leaves of red cabbage in a blender. Boil the mixture for 10 minutes, and then strain the cabbage juice into a container. Put 1 tablespoon (15 milliliters) of the cabbage juice indicator into several plastic or glass cups. Add some lemon juice to one of the cups. It will turn reddish pink because lemon juice is acidic.

Add some liquid soap to one of the cups. It will turn blue because liquid soaps are bases. Try other household liquids, such as ammonia or orange juice.

Bases are slippery and taste bitter, while acids, like lemon juice or vinegar, taste sour. DO NOT taste anything that you are not certain is a food. Many acids and bases, even those found in household supplies, are extremely toxic.

The Tide Pod challenge has been in the news lately. The Tide Pod challenge involves biting into a detergent packet, which has a candy-like appearance, and either spitting out or consuming its poisonous contents. This foolish stunt can lead to an array of serious health problems, including burns to the mouth, esophagus, and respiratory tract. Some people have been rushed to the hospital after experiencing cognitive issues. Ingesting Tide Pods can lead to vomiting and diarrhea. Best to stick with candy!

Try making your own litmus paper. Soak 6-inch by 1-inch (15-centimeter by 2.5-centimeter) strips of coffee filter in the cabbage juice for one minute and let them dry. Try your litmus paper on apple juice, Rolaids, Pepto-Bismol, Listerine, vinegar, lemon juice, and baking soda. Your homemade litmus strip will turn color based on the pH.

Sodium hydroxide would be about the highest level on the pH scale with about a 14. Household bleach is very basic with a pH close to 14. Hydrochloric acid has a pH of near zero. Gastric acid and lemon juice have a pH around one or two. Urine is about a six, slightly acidic. Blood is around 7.4, a bit basic.

Q91: How do X-rays take pictures of our bones?

X-rays are a kind of light, but a light we can't see. Other types of light waves that we can't see are radio and television waves, gamma rays, ultraviolet, and infrared. Stars, including our own sun, give off X-rays. Our atmosphere prevents most of the X-rays from reaching the surface of the earth.

X-rays are very short waves and have a lot more energy than visible light waves. X-rays have so much energy they can penetrate most anything: wood, glass, water, muscles, and skin. Light waves bounce right off skin, but high-energy X-rays push right through it. Bone is much denser than skin, fat, and muscles. Most X-rays stop when they encounter bone. Just as we could take a picture of a fish in water, X-rays can take pictures of bones through skin and muscle.

Let's say the doctor wants to take an X-ray of your leg to see if it is broken. Your leg is sandwiched between an X-ray machine and a piece of film that has never been exposed to any light. The X-ray machine is fired up. The X-rays pass through the skin, fat, and muscle and then travel on to expose the film. Many are stopped by bone. When the X-ray film is developed, it shows an outline of the bones. If a bone is cracked or broken, some X-rays make it through the crack or the break and unto the film. The doctor can see that the bone is broken.

X-rays damage cells and can cause great harm. That's why the doctor takes as few X-rays as necessary. The technicians who operate the X-ray machines see many patients a day. Their exposure can be quite high, so they stand behind a lead-lined door while taking X-rays. Lead is so dense it stops virtually all X-rays. Patients are also protected by wearing lead-filled garments to limit exposure of areas of the body that are not being X-rayed. The beams for dental and medical X-rays are carefully controlled.

X-rays can also be used to image tiny objects, such as individual molecules. Hints to the physical structure of DNA were found via X-rays. Complex proteins like insulin have been studied by means of X-rays. X-rays have also been used to find the outline of an earlier painting in a canvas that has been painted over.

X-rays are produced by shooting electrons at a metal target. Wilhelm Röntgen discovered X-rays quite by accident in 1895 while experimenting with vacuum tubes. Röntgen called the new rays X, like the unknown in algebra. A week later, he took an X-ray of his wife's hand, showing the bones and the wedding ring on her finger. When his wife saw her own bones, she cried out, "I have seen my own death." Wilhelm Röntgen won the Nobel Prize in Physics in 1901 for his discovery of X-rays.

Famous scientists Thomas Edison and Nikola Tesla experimented with X-rays. But the greatest advances in X-ray technology came about during World War I. Madame Curie, awarded the Nobel Prize in Physics in 1903 and the Nobel Prize in Chemistry in 1911, recognized that wounded soldiers were best served if operated upon as soon as possible. She oversaw the installation of 20 mobile X-ray units and 200 X-ray units in field hospitals in the first year of the war.

Q92: *How does a compound differ from an element?*
· ·

I n the world of chemistry, there are elements, compounds, atoms, molecules, and mixtures. Let's try to sort them out.

Elements are pure chemical substances made of one single type of atom. Every element has a symbol. Examples of elements are hydrogen (H), iron (Fe), and copper (Cu). There are 94 elements that occur in nature and about 24 artificially produced when undergoing radioactive changes.

Elements are noted by their name, symbol, atomic number, melting point, boiling point, and density. Elements are arranged in the periodic table by their atomic number or Z number, which is the number of protons in each atom's nucleus. Elements cannot be broken down into simpler substances by chemical reactions and can't be separated chemically. In the periodic table, they are grouped according to similar chemical properties and are shown by their symbols.

Take carbon as an example. Carbon has six protons in the nucleus, so it has an atomic number of six. Carbon also has six neutrons in the nucleus. Add the 6 protons in the nucleus and 6 neutrons in the nucleus and we have 12 particles in the nucleus. This is called the atomic mass, or weight, or the A number. For carbon, the Z number is 6 and the A number is 12. The term *carbon-12* is often used.

Sometimes an element can have extra neutrons in the nucleus. Carbon can have 7 neutrons instead of the normal 6, or even 8 neutrons in the nucleus. There can be a carbon-13 or carbon-14. Such alternate versions of atoms are called isotopes. Carbon-14 is useful in finding the age of once living material such as bones, wood, or papyrus.

Some isotopes are radioactive and provide a great benefit in medical procedures and industrial applications. Iodine-131 is commonly used to treat thyroid cancer. Strontium-89 and samarium-153 fight bone cancer. Americium-141 is used in smoke detectors. Thallium-204 helps measure and regulate the thickness of materials coming off a milling machine.

A compound has two or more kinds of atoms that are combined in fixed ratios, arranged in a defined manner through chemical bonds. The smallest unit of a compound is one of these multi-atom molecules. Compounds can be chemically separated or broken apart into simpler substances by chemical methods or reactions. Every compound has a formula that tells us what elements make it up and in what proportion. Examples of compounds are water (H_2O), sodium bicarbonate ($NaHCO_3$), and sodium chloride (NaCl). This tells us, for example, that one atom of sodium (Na) combines with one atom of chlorine (Cl) to form one molecule of sodium chloride (NaCl) compound, or common table salt. The elements of sodium and chlorine combine by sharing their outer electrons.

Molecule is a general term used to describe atoms connected by chemical bonds. Every combination of atoms is a molecule. In addition to salt being a molecule, we can consider water to be a molecule because it is made of two atoms of hydrogen (H) and one of oxygen (O). Even oxygen itself usually exists as a molecule, with two oxygen atoms bound together (the oxygen we breathe) or even three atoms bound together (ozone).

Unlike a compound, a mixture is all about physical properties, not chemical properties. You could put salt in water and stir it up and dissolve the salt. You now have a mixture, but both the salt (NaCl) and water (H_2O) keep their own chemical properties. If you boiled off the water, the salt would remain. Or you could spread out the mixture, and the water would eventually evaporate (a kind of boiling) away, leaving the salt. Two liquids can also be a mixture. If oil and water are mixed, the denser water will settle to the bottom by gravity, leaving the less dense oil on top.

Benzene is an organic chemical molecule composed of six carbon atoms in a ring, with one hydrogen atom attached to each carbon atom. Benzene is a natural component of crude oil. It is colorless, has a sweet smell, and is highly flammable. So perhaps you heard about this guy who threw a lighted match in a pail of this volatile hydrocarbon and hasn't benzene since.

Q93: *What is an alloy?*

An alloy is a mixture of metals. Metals are marvelous servants and remarkably useful, but not in their pure form. Pure gold used in jewelry is worthless, as it is so soft that it bends and scratches with normal handling. Jewelry gold is mixed, or alloyed, with silver or copper to make it stronger. Most gold jewelry is not 24 carats (100 percent pure), but is 18 carats, a much stronger alloy consisting of 75 percent gold.

Alloys are made when elements are mixed in the molten state. The mixture is then allowed to cool and solidify. Most often, metals in alloys must have similar-sized ions (charged atoms) and a similar number of free electrons. The ions of one metal can replace ions in the other metal. Basically, the electrons in the outer orbits of each element are free to move about and settle into a lattice or crystalline structure.

There are exceptions. Sometimes a metal can be mixed with a non-metal. A notable example is when a small bit of carbon (non-metal) is mixed with pure, soft iron (metal).The holes in the iron lattice structure are filled with carbon atoms to form the extremely strong and versatile steel. Steel occupies the number one rating for usefulness of alloys.

The world's oldest alloy is bronze, a mixture of copper and tin. Bronze revolutionized weapon and tool making. It ushered in the Bronze Age, which began about 3000 BCE. The Bronze Age is the second part of the three-age system for classifying prehistoric societies—Stone, Bronze, Iron. Bronze can easily be cast. When molten, it flows readily into every part of a mold.

Another common alloy is brass, made by mixing copper and zinc. The hardness property of brass is determined by varying the proportions of copper and zinc. Modern brass contains small portions of silicon, aluminum, phosphorus, and arsenic. Prized for its gold-like appearance, brass is used for decoration. Its low surface friction makes it valuable for gears, locks, and bearings. Brass musical instruments are common. Brass will not spark easily when struck, a nice feature for fittings and tools used around explosive gases.

Dental amalgams, mixtures of liquid mercury and a powdered alloy of silver, copper, and tin, have been used for more than 150 years. They are known as silver fillings because of the color.

Aluminum is widely employed in aircraft construction because it is lightweight and strong. However, it comes up short in its ability to withstand stresses and temperature changes. Airplane aluminum must be alloyed with small quantities of copper, magnesium, iron, nickel, and silicon to give the desired properties. In high-speed aircraft, such as the SR-71 spy plane, titanium is used instead because it can withstand high temperatures.

All modern coins are metal alloys, combinations of gold, silver, nickel, copper, and zinc. The U.S. penny is about 97 percent zinc, with a 3 percent copper cladding. When nickel is added to copper, an alloy termed *cupronickel* is produced. Our U.S nickel is 25 percent nickel and 75 percent copper. The dime, quarter, and half-dollar are all about 8.3 percent nickel and 91.7 percent copper.

Cupronickel (copper and nickel) is highly resistant to corrosion. Some iron and manganese are added for strengthening. Cupronickel is ideal for seawater pipes, heat exchangers, propellers, crankshafts, and hulls of boats.

Q94: *Why are some elements radioactive?*
· ·

S ome elements are radioactive because they are unstable. Atoms have a central core called the nucleus. The nucleus is made up of protons, with a positive charge, and neutrons that do not have a charge. They are neutral, as the name implies. Orbiting the nucleus are tiny negative electrons.

In that nucleus are those protons, all with a positive charge. Protons repel protons, since "like" charges repel. The nucleus wants to fly apart. But the neutrons prevent that from happening. The neutrons stick to the protons using a fundamental force called the strong nuclear force. The neutrons keep the protons from flying apart.

There are two competing forces at work: one pulling and one pushing. For most atoms, there are just enough neutrons to keep the nucleus stable. But for some atoms, such as uranium and plutonium, the ratio of neutrons to protons is out of whack.

Nature wants the radioactive atom to become stable, so it throws off some pieces of itself. This ejection, or throwing off, is called radioactivity. There are three kinds of radioactivity depending on what is thrown off.

An alpha particle is ejected when there are too many protons in the nucleus. It is made of two protons and two neutrons. It's a massive particle, as particles go, and carries a positive charge. It can't travel very far and can be stopped by 1 inch (2.5 centimeters) of air or a piece of paper. It's harmless outside the body but can be deadly if it gets inside a person.

A beta particle is an electron ejected from an atom when there are too many neutrons in the nucleus. One of the atoms neutrons changes into a proton. A beta particle has a negative charge. Beta particles can be stopped by a thin sheet of metal.

The third type of radiation is the gamma ray. Gamma radiation happens when there is too much energy in the nucleus. It's not a particle but a wave, much like a light wave or a radio or television wave, but at a much higher frequency or vibration rate. Gamma rays can be stopped by thick metal, deep water, several feet of soil, or a lead shield.

All three of these types of radiation can be dangerous because they pack a terrific wallop due to their high speed. The kinetic energy of these particles is sufficient to smash apart chemical structures in the human body. A strong dose can damage DNA and cause cancer. A really robust attack can burn the skin, destroy blood cells, and kill within minutes.

We get hit by radioactive particles all day and every day. They are in such small amounts that they don't do much harm. Still, people do have to be careful about radiation. There is an insidious nature to radiation. Certain kinds of radioactive particles can be absorbed, and our body will treat them just like chemicals that we are used to.

Radioactive Iodine-131 replaces the regular iodine in the thyroid. Cesium-137 and Strontium-90 replace calcium in the bone. Plutonium-239 can replace iron in the blood and bone marrow.

There are a number of good ways that science has used radiation. These include X-rays, carbon dating, nuclear power plants, and killing germs. Radiation therapy is one of the most common treatments for cancer. It uses high-energy particles or waves, such as X-rays, gamma rays, electron beams, or protons, to destroy or damage cancer cells.

Like many things in life, radiation has pluses and minuses. Radioactive elements can kill or cure.

Q95: How can carbon dating tell us how old things are?

R emember Ötzi, the Iceman, found by hikers at 10,500-feet (3,200-meter) altitude in Switzerland in September 1991? He is the oldest known preserved natural mummy in Europe. Ötzi has been examined, X-rayed, and carbon dated. About the year 3300 BCE, he became frozen in the glacial ice. Ötzi was 65 inches (1.7 meters) tall and weighed in at 110 pounds (49.9 kilograms). Scientists know what he was eating up to the time of his demise. His clothes, shoes, and weapons have been extensively examined. In 2001, a CT scan showed that poor Ötzi had an arrowhead lodged in this left shoulder and most likely died from loss of blood.

A young lady, called the Inca Ice Maiden, was found atop a mountain in southern Peru in 1995. She caused a sensation in the scientific world because of how well her body, clothes, and belongings were preserved in the icy world near 20,000 feet (6,096 meters) altitude. She was 13 years old at the time of her death. She was killed by a blunt trauma blow to the head as a human sacrifice to the Inca gods. Carbon-14 dating places her death sometime between CE 1450 and 1480, almost 600 years ago.

We know much about Ötzi and the Inca Ice Maiden because of radiocarbon dating. Carbon is one of the most plentiful elements on Earth, found in our bodies, in pencils, coal, and diamonds. Carbon exits in two main forms: carbon-12 and the less common and less stable carbon-14. Carbon-12 has 6 protons (positive particles) and 6 neutrons (neutral particles) in the nucleus. Add the protons and neutrons to get an atomic mass or atomic weight of 12.

Carbon-14 is created high in the atmosphere when cosmic rays knock neutrons out of atomic nuclei. These wild neutrons, now moving fast, hit ordinary nitrogen at lower altitudes. A neutron enters the nitrogen nucleus and knocks out a proton. This converts nitrogen-14 (7 protons and 7 neutrons) into carbon-14 (6 protons and 8 neutrons.)

The extra two neutrons make the carbon atom unstable. The atom is said to be radioactive. Any radioactive atom wants to become stable by throwing off particles and rays.

Carbon-12 and carbon-14 are present in a set ratio in all living things. When they die, the carbon-14 decays at a steady, unvarying rate. The word *decay* does not refer to "rot" as in decaying organic matter. It means changing from one element to another. When a plant or animal dies, it stops interacting with the biosphere and does not take in any additional carbon-14 from the air or food. The carbon-14 atoms that decay are no longer replaced, so the amount of carbon-14 in that once-living thing decreases as time goes on. It reduces at a steady rate as the ratio of carbon-14 to carbon-12 gets smaller. Carbon-14 dating can be considered a type of atomic clock that starts ticking the moment something dies.

The steady rate for carbon-14 is 5,730 years, which is said to be the half-life. After 5,730 years, only half of the original carbon-14 is left. After another 5,730 years, or 11,460 years, only one fourth, or a quarter, of the original amount is left. After three half-lives (17,190 years) only one eighth remains.

Radiocarbon dating, as it is often called, is only accurate back to about 50,000 years ago. After that amount of time, hardly any carbon-14 remains. Corrections must be made for the varying amounts of carbon-14 in the atmosphere, which can change due to atomic testing, volcanic activity, and massive burning of fossil fuels. Carbon dating can only be used on things that once lived. It can't determine the age of rocks, or volcanic output, or the age of the earth. Age of rocks and such are determined by the ratio of uranium to lead and similar techniques.

Radiocarbon dating was discovered and perfected right after World War II by Willard Libby, while he was working at the University of California Radiation Laboratory in Berkeley and later at the University of Chicago. Dr. Libby was awarded the Nobel Prize in Chemistry in 1960 for his work.

Radiocarbon dating is a marvelous tool for the archaeologist and paleontologist. The Dead Sea Scrolls, discovered in a cave by a Bedouin shepherd in 1947, are a prime example. Most of the Dead Sea Scrolls were written on goat and calf hides, and some on linen that came from flax plants. All are organic material and hence can be dated. The fragments range in age from 400 BCE to CE 400. The best proof of the accuracy of carbon dating is when the age of the material dated can be matched to the dates of historical events and people known to have lived at the time. The Dead Sea Scrolls proved that carbon dating is quite precise.

Chapter Eleven

How the World Works

Q96: *How does a pendulum work?*

G ravity is what makes a pendulum work. A simple pendulum is a device that consists of a weight (called a bob) on the end of a rod, string, or flexible tether. When pulled back to put it in motion, the pendulum swings back and forth. The time needed for one complete swing is called a period. The period depends only on the length of the pendulum. The amount of weight on the end of the rod or string does not change how long the pendulum takes to make one full swing. The distance you pull the weight back also makes essentially no difference in the period of the pendulum.

Pendulums are used to regulate the timing of grandfather clocks. The bob can be moved up or down on the rod to adjust the working length of the pendulum and thus the timing of the clock. Most grandfather clocks have a pendulum that changes its length to compensate for temperature changes. Metals expand or get longer when they are warm and get shorter when they are cold. So if the grandfather clock is not compensated for temperature differences, the clock will not give accurate timing.

You can make yourself part of a pendulum. Just sit in a swing and start yourself going. If you have long ropes or chains, the time for one swing (period) is long. If the ropes or chains are short, the time is short. Metronomes that are used to time music often use an inverted pendulum.

Galileo is credited with the discovery of the relationship between the length of a pendulum and the time of the swing (period). Galileo sat in church and observed the swinging of a great lamp. He used the beat of his pulse as a clock. He found the time for one swing is less by one half if the length of the pendulum is one fourth the original length.

What length of pendulum do you need so that the period is one second? You might try this experiment.

Tie a 2-foot (61-centimeter) long string to some kind of weight, such as a rock, nut, or washer. Use a piece of tape to temporarily attach the other end of the string to the edge of a table. Pull the pendulum weight back several inches and let it swing to and fro.

Count the number of swings in one minute. Remember, a swing means all the way over and back. If you get more or fewer than 60 swings in one minute, adjust the length. Will you have to make your string longer or shorter? Keep adjusting the length so that you have 60 swings in 60 seconds. When that happens, you have made a pendulum that has a period of one second.

Q97: *What is an atomic clock?*

C locks have come a long way from the days of the grandfather clock that keeps time by the steady back-and-forth oscillations of a pendulum. The pendulum is powered by falling weights. Many old-time clocks used a balance wheel alternating backward and forward. Power was provided by a wound spring. Quartz watches depend on the vibrating oscillations of a crystal. Power is furnished by a battery.

An atomic clock should really be labeled "radio-controlled clock." When you buy a clock labeled "atomic clock" you are buying one that can be synchronized to the US official atomic clock in Boulder, Colorado. These clocks and wristwatches can pick up the radio transmissions of broadcast stations on several frequencies.

The National Institute of Standards and Technology (NIST) airs time signals on powerful transmitters on radio station WWV from Fort Collins, Colorado, and WWVH from Kauai, Hawaii. The frequencies are 2.5, 5, 10, 15, and 20 MHz. Reception of any radio signal can be affected by weather, terrain, location, time of day, time of year, and atmospheric and ionosphere conditions. Using so many frequencies ensures reception anywhere in the world for at least part of the day.

The radio receiver is tiny, about the size of tip of pencil, and can easily be imbedded in computer chips or utilized in GPS units and cell phones. The miniature receiver need only pick up the radio transmission once each few days to do the job of correcting any error in the receiver's clock. Generally, the clock-updating will take place at night when the signal is strongest. Many home automation devices, including computers connected to the Internet, are continually and automatically updated to the correct time.

WWV sends a digital time code on 60 KHz that modulates or changes the power of the carrier signal picked up by the receiving antenna. The receiver decodes the bits to get the time, the day of the year, daylight saving time, and leap-year indicators. WWV reports what is called the Coordinated Universal Time.

Atomic clocks, the kind used by NIST, go back to 1945 when physicist Isidor Rabi determined that atoms maintain a steady unchanging vibration rate that is more precise than the pendulum, balance wheel, or quartz crystal. Early atomic clocks used the vibration of ammonia molecules, but today's atomic clocks go with cesium. Estimates vary as to the accuracy. One scientist claims precision to within one second in 126 years. Another report puts it at one second in 30 million years. Either one will get you to the church on time!

The NIST has the big expensive atomic clocks that generate extremely accurate time signals, and you and I can buy inexpensive atomic clocks that are synchronized to the government atomic clocks. Listen in on WWV on any one of the frequencies listed above on any shortwave radio receiver. The 15 and 20 MHz signals are strongest during the day. The 5 MHz and 10 MHz come in best at night. You hear the study tick, tick, tick, and then a human voice announces the time on the minute. It's quite amazing!

Q98: When you look at the front side of a spoon, why is your reflection upside down, while on the back side, it's right side up?

· ·

A spoon is a curved mirror. What you see is the image made when light bounces off your face, off the mirror, and then back to your eye. If you are looking into a flat mirror, the light will come straight back to you. Not so with a curved mirror. When light bounces off a curved mirror, it won't come straight back to you, but will come back at an angle instead. Light rays travel in a straight line until they hit something. A light ray comes straight back only when it hits something straight on. If the surface of the object is slanted relative to the light, it will cause the light to be reflected at an angle.

If you look at the front of the spoon, it is a concave mirror. Your image can be either smaller or larger than in a straight mirror. The key is how close you are to the mirror. If you are really close, your image is right side up and large. As you back up from the mirror the image gets smaller and flips upside down.

Dentists use concave mirrors to examine teeth. These mirrors make your teeth look bigger so the dentists can examine them more easily. Shaving mirrors and make-up mirrors are concave to make the face look bigger. Concave mirrors are used in reflecting telescopes, such as the famous Hubble Space Telescope orbiting Earth.

The back side of the spoon is a convex mirror. Convex mirrors make things look smaller and never reverse the image upside down. Convex mirrors are used in factories and stores to see down the aisles, or on the passenger side of cars to prevent blind spots. These mirrors are often etched with the warning "Objects in mirror are closer than they appear."

Q99: How do airplanes measure their speed through the air?

Airplanes have a metal tube, called a pitot (PEE-toe) tube, that goes from outside the airplane to an instrument called the airspeed indicator. Henri Pitot, French engineer, invented the device in the early 1700s to measure the velocity of gases.

As a plane is flying, the onrushing air goes into the open pitot tube and causes a flexible metal diaphragm in the airspeed instrument to expand. The faster the plane goes, the more the diaphragm expands. The diaphragm expansion is converted by mechanical linkage to move a dial on the front of the gauge, so the pilot can read how fast the plane is moving through the air.

A heating element is incorporated with the pitot tube on most all aircraft to prevent the tube from clogging with ice or snow. On December 1, 1974, a Northwest Orient Boeing 727 was on its way to Buffalo, New York, to pick up the Baltimore Colts football team. The three crew members onboard were killed when the aircraft flew too slowly, stalled, and spun into the ground. They had failed to turn on the pitot heat system and received the wrong readings on their airspeed indicator.

More recently, in 2009, an Airbus A330 operated by Air France crashed into the Atlantic Ocean on a flight from Rio de Janeiro, Brazil, to Paris, France. With a loss of 216 passengers and 12 crew members, it was the deadliest in French history. Two years after the accident, the plane's black boxes were recovered. The plane had flown through the edges of thunderstorms, and the aircraft's pitot tubes were obstructed by ice crystals. The crew received erroneous airspeed readings. The autopilot became disconnected and the crew had difficulty flying the aircraft manually.

Of all the instruments on any aircraft, the airspeed indicator is considered the most important.

Q100: *How does a zipper work?*
· ·

The zipper was patented in 1893 by Whitcomb Judson as a method to fasten boots. The US Navy bought Judson's patent in 1918 to secure flying suits. His invention was given the name zipper in 1926.

The zipper is an excellent example of a simple machine. All machinery, implements, and instruments are made up of six simple machines—the lever, pulley, wheel and axle, inclined plane, wedge, and screw. The zipper makes use of the wedge, which is really a form of an inclined plane, to bring together two sets of interlocking teeth. David Macaulay's wonderful book *The Way Things Work* shows that the slide of a zipper contains wedges that either force the interlocking teeth together or force them apart.

The teeth are built so that they can only be opened or closed one at a time. The slide is necessary to pull the teeth apart or put them together. To open the zipper, the upper wedge forces the teeth apart one at a time. To close the zipper, the wedge forces the interlocking teeth together, making them intermesh.

Each tooth has a small knob or protrusion on its top face and a hollow on its bottom. Teeth on opposite sides of the zipper are staggered so that the protrusion of one fits into the hollow of the opposite tooth on the adjoining side. Some plastic zippers use two intermeshing spirals instead of two rows of teeth.

Try this simple science experiment to see how a wedge works. Press the eraser end of a pencil against a sheet of cardboard. Note that it is nearly impossible to push the pencil eraser through the cardboard. Now stick the sharp point of the pencil into the cardboard. The pencil point acts as a wedge, which has a tapered thin, pie-shaped edge. The point of the pencil penetrates the cardboard and creates a path for the bigger part of the pencil to follow.

Wedges are used to split logs. The teeth of saws are wedges. All knife blades are wedges.

Q101: *Why do wires spark when you plug something in?*

Wires that spark when you plug something in are normal and quite harmless. Let's use a table lamp as an example. A perfectly normal two-prong plug, or a three-prong plug, will sometimes spark when plugged into a wall socket if the lamp switch is closed or "on."

Why is that? The closed circuit in the switch means that the last open connection in the circuit will be at the point where the plug meets the wall socket. The plug and socket are the final links in the chain that will let the current flow. This open circuit as it is being closed may cause an arc to jump across the air gap in the last fraction of an inch. Generally, the spark caused by this occurrence is quite harmless. If you want to avoid the spark, you should turn off whatever lamp or appliance you are using before you put the plug into the wall socket.

If a lamp is already plugged in and someone turns on the switch, a spark jumps inside the switch. That's what switches are designed to handle. Many switches have mechanical springs that quickly snap the switch open or closed even if you move it slowly.

The spark or electric arc will be larger if there is a bigger load. For example, there is a bigger spark if the lamp is 100 watts rather than 25 watts. A high-wattage halogen lamp is more likely to create a spark than an incandescent lamp. An electric heater is often 1,000 watts or more. An electric heater will experience a spark, whereas a radio will not. Also, if the load or appliance has an inductive motor, such as a vacuum cleaner, expect an arc. Again, a spark may occur if the vacuum cleaner switch has already been turned on before plugging it in.

There are a few small electronic devices that will spark when plugged in, even when turned off. These devices contain capacitors that store electricity and charge up when first plugged in. That brief burst of power may cause a momentary spark. Devices such as computer power supplies or flat screen TVs contain capacitors.

The same spark phenomenon may happen when any lamp or appliance is unplugged from a wall socket. Again, it will occur only when the appliance or lamp is "on" or operating.

What is this electric spark that jumps from metal plug to metal socket? A spark is the moving of an electric charge, or current, through air. Air is an insulator and conducts electricity poorly. Still, if the electric field exceeds a certain value, the air gets ionized and becomes highly conductive, enabling the charge to move. An electric field occurs around any charge, just as a magnetic field surrounds a magnet, and a gravitational field surrounds a mass.

Where does the light of the spark come from? So much current can flow through that very tiny gap between plug and socket that the temperature of the air can rise to several thousand degrees. The air turns to plasma or ionized gas, and the metal on the tip of the plug turns to vapor. With those high temperatures comes the emission of light. It's a tiny lightning bolt. You may hear a pop sound. That's the thunder.

It is amazing how much science is involved in the plugging and unplugging of lights and appliances. Oddly enough, a spark across a gap of conductors is the basis of the carbon arc lamp. Carbon arc lamps provided the only electric light available to light large areas for a hundred years, from 1800 to 1901. An arc lamp works by hooking two carbon rods to a source of electricity. With the other ends of the rods spaced at the right distance, electrical current will flow through an "arc" of vaporizing carbon, creating an intense white light capable of lighting a large length of street or a large factory interior. It was cheaper to light streets with the arc lamp than gas or oil lamps. Carbon arc was utilized as the light for movie projectors in theaters for many years.

Here is some general advice from electricians. Any socket that shows burned or blackened marks should be replaced. Water can cause an outlet to spark. Outlets known as ground fault circuit interrupters (GFCI) will cause a circuit to shut down rather than flowing along an unintended path, such as through water or a person. GFCI can be tricky to install properly, so it's prudent to let a professional handle it. A plug, outlet, or cord should never become hot or emit smoke or odors.

Chapter Twelve

Stuff I Always Wondered About

Q102: *Why do living things have to die?*
. . . .

T hings wear out. Our bodies wear out. Aging is a natural occurrence and not a disease. There seems to be two aspects to aging: nature (genetic influences) and nurture (environmental influences). Aging is to a large extent under genetic control. Many scientists say that we are genetically programmed to die in less than 100 years.

Even cells of our body have different life spans. Stomach cells last about 2 days, red blood cells 120 days, bone cells about 30 years, and brain cells last a lifetime. Still, the organism, as a whole, has a limited lifespan.

No matter how well we take care of ourselves, our bodies wear out, shut down, and die. There is another aspect to aging—the nurture or environmental part. It involves the accumulation of changes or mutations. These lead to loss of metabolic capacity. With time, muscle and skin cells slowly lose their ability to regenerate.

The good news is that we do have some control over the aging process. Good diet, moderate use of alcohol, avoidance of tobacco, avoidance of overexposure to the sun's ultraviolet (UV) rays, and an exercise regimen all contribute to slowing the aging process.

American men live about 76 years and women around 81 years on average. The leading cause of death in the United States is heart disease (one out of three people) and cancer (one out of four). Dread infectious diseases, such as polio, typhoid, smallpox, and diphtheria, have been conquered, so accidents are now the leading cause of death for people under 21.

Do we really want people to live forever? Think of the overpopulation. Think of the lines at McDonald's!

How long do things last? A sequoia tree will live for 2,500 years. A mouse lives two years. A housefly has a lifespan of 25 days. A facelift is good for 10 years. A pencil will write 30,000 words. A dollar bill is in circulation for 18 months.

There are some people who are very reluctant to let go. Six billionaires out in California's Silicon Valley have invested millions of dollars into researching the aging process and longevity development. Peter Thiel, cofounder of PayPal; Larry Ellison, founder of Oracle; Larry Page, cofounder of Google; and Mark Zuckerberg, cofounder of Facebook are a few of the well-known moguls who want to extend their lives beyond the normal lifespan.

Q103: *How is sound created when two things collide?*

All sounds are caused by rapid motion of air. When things collide, they vibrate, flexing back and forth. When a piece of material flexes out on one side, it pushes the surrounding air particles on that side. These molecules of air collide with the molecules in front of them and so on. This compression of air travels to our ear and pushes our eardrum inward.

When the material flexes the other way, it pulls in the surrounding air molecules, creating a partial vacuum. This pressure decrease is called a rarefaction, and when it travels to our ear it causes the eardrum to move outward. These compressions and rarefactions, and the resulting movement of our eardrum, are what we perceive as sound.

Most of the energy of any collision goes into heat energy. Even the bouncing of a ball on the floor causes the ball and floor to heat up slightly. But some of the energy of motion, called kinetic energy, goes into sound energy. The amount of the kinetic energy that goes into sound energy depends on the types of material, the speed of the collision, and the structural makeup of the colliding materials. For example, a bullet hitting a tree would be much quieter than the same bullet hitting a metal plate. The tree doesn't vibrate very much, but the metal plate does.

The rate at which objects vibrate is known as the frequency and is given by the unit called hertz. One hertz is one cycle or back-and-forth vibration per second—too low for us to hear. In music, we use the term *tone* or *pitch*. An object that vibrates at a higher rate has a higher frequency and higher pitch. The amplitude determines how loudly the sound is perceived.

Sound level or amplitude of sound waves is given in decibels (dB). The ear can hear over a very large range. The sound of a jet engine is a trillion times more powerful than the least audible sound. A trillion is a one with 12 zeros.

Decibels are expressed in logarithmic units. A barely audible sound is 0 (zero) dB. A sound 10 times more powerful is 10 dB. A sound 1,000 times more powerful compared to 0 dB is 30 dB. That's how the logarithmic decibel scale works. Normal conversation occurs at 60 dB. A car horn is more than 100 dB. Anything above 85 dB can cause hearing damage. Much depends on the duration of exposure. The threshold of pain is 120 dB. At that level, most people must cover their ears. It's about the same as being at a rock concert!

Q104: Why do people wear glasses with different kinds of lenses?

The two most common defects of human vision are nearsightedness and farsightedness. The job of glasses or contact lenses is to bend or refract light to form a sharp image on the retina.

The action of our eye is similar to the operation of a camera. Light that comes through the lens of the camera forms an image on film. You can focus the camera by moving the lens closer to or further from the film.

The eye's cornea and lens allow light to form an image on the retina. The eye obtains a sharp image on the retina by having the lens change its shape. Various factors influence how good a job the eye can do in forming that sharp image. Those factors include eyeball shape, muscle movement, age, elasticity, and lens opening.

Young people who need to wear glasses are usually nearsighted. They have no problem doing close-up work such as reading or typing. They have difficulty seeing things that are far away, such as a school blackboard, a television, or street signs. The eyeball of a nearsighted person is too long, so the image is focused before it gets to the retina. A concave lens, thinner in the middle, is needed to spread the light out to form an image on the retina.

Older people who wear glasses are most often farsighted. They have problems seeing things that are close to them. You sometimes see older people holding their newspapers at arm's length because they have no problem seeing things that are far away. The eye's lens becomes stiffer with age and cannot flex sufficiently to focus on something close. Farsighted people need a convex lens that is thicker in the middle that will converge, or bring light rays in.

Try this easy science experiment if you want to find out if a friend is nearsighted or farsighted. Borrow your friend's eyeglasses. Hold the glasses up to the sun and let the light shine through the lenses and onto a sheet of typing paper. Move the paper toward and away from the lens to form a sharp image. If the eyeglass lenses bring the sun's light together to form a bright spot, then that person is farsighted. Most likely the lenses are from an older person that is at least middle-aged (let's say around 60). If the eyeglass lenses spread the sun's ray out to form a darker image on the paper with a brighter border around the dark image, then that person is nearsighted. The eyeglasses probably belong to a younger person.

Q105: What was the first radio broadcasting station?

That distinction goes to KDKA in Pittsburgh. The Westinghouse station broadcast the November 2, 1920, presidential election results between Warren G. Harding and James M. Cox. Harding won. Station KDKA was the first to use electron tube technology that sent a crystal-clear signal. It was the first station to sell commercials and the first station to be licensed outside the amateur bands.

KDKA is an AM (amplitude modulation) clear channel station. Amplitude modulation is the broadcast mode in which the height or amplitude of the carrier signal is changed by the voice or music being aired. Clear channel means that no other station broadcasts on their 1020 KHz frequency. KDKA can use the maximum power of 50,000 watts.

In Chicago, Illinois, WGN is a clear channel AM station on 720 KHz that can be heard all over the Midwest and much of the nation. WSM (620 KHz) in Nashville, Tennessee, is another such clear channel. They broadcast the Grand Ole Opry. At night, AM radio signals bounce off a layer of the sky called the ionosphere. This "skip" allows one to hear stations hundreds of miles away.

A huge advantage of AM is that the broadcast signal can be detected, decoded, and heard with very simple equipment. Many a kid built a crystal radio receiver in the 1930s, 1940s, and even the 1950s.

The foxhole or POW (prisoner of war) radio was built from whatever materials the World War II American soldiers could scrounge. A razor blade, lengths of wire, headset or earphone, safety pin, pencil, and a board to mount it on, and they were in business. The razor blade and pencil lead acted as the detector or gate. When the steel razor blade and lead came in contact with each other, electricity flowed in one direction. The path was from steel to lead, then into the headphones. The foxhole radio did not need any power supply. The power came from the radio signal itself. There are accounts of POWs in Japan and GIs in Italy building and using these simple radio receivers.

If AM enjoys the advantage of simple receivers, it has a drawback. The signal is subject to interference from storms and electrical wiring. FM (frequency modulation) is not subject to atmospheric disturbances. However, the receiver is more complex.

Radio stations east of the Mississippi River start with the letter W, as in WOR in New York. Stations west of the Mississippi River start with a K as in KSPN in Los Angeles. There are some exceptions to this rule.

Q106: Why is asbestos bad for a person?
. . . .

Asbestos is a generic term for a group of natural occurring minerals that have been mined and used in construction, industry, and the military since the 1880s. The big advantage to using asbestos is its resistance to heat and combustion. Asbestos has superb insulating and soundproofing properties in addition to being quite cheap.

The biggest producers of asbestos are Russia, China, Brazil, and Canada. Asbestos is still used in many developing countries. It has been widely used in building materials and pipe insulation, brake linings, floor tile, shingles, firefighter's clothing, mats, fiber cement, and fire-resistant bricks.

There are different types of asbestos, the most common being white asbestos (chrysotile) found in cement products, insulation, and auto and truck brake linings. White asbestos is also resistant to salt water, hence its popularity in ship construction.

But asbestos can be dangerous to human health. Asbestos fibers are extremely small, about one fifth the diameter of a human hair. The fibers can easily become airborne and inhaled into the lungs where they remain permanently. In the lungs, the fibers do their damage. Asbestosis is scarring of the lungs that restricts one's ability to inhale. Breathing becomes more and more difficult, until the lungs become useless. Asbestos exposure can also lead to mesothelioma, which is cancer of the lung lining. The combination of smoking and exposure to asbestos also greatly increases the risk of developing lung cancer.

People who get asbestosis and mesothelioma generally have been exposed to the material for long periods of time and in high concentrations. Shipbuilders and certain factory workers fall into this category. The symptoms may not appear until 20 to 30 years after the first exposures. No safe exposure limit has ever been determined. However, the longer the period of exposure an individual experiences, the greater the risk.

Thousands of tons of asbestos were used in World War II ships to wrap pipes, line boilers, and cover engines. There were 4.3 million shipyard workers in the United States during the war. Estimates are that for every thousand workers about 14 died of mesothelioma. An unknown number died from asbestosis.

Friability is a word you'll hear when asbestos removal is being discussed. Friability is the ability of a solid material to be reduced to smaller pieces with very little effort. Asbestos may be friable if small particles are easily dislodged, enabling them to become small enough to become airborne and to be inhaled into the lungs.

Most products manufactured in the United States today do not contain asbestos. Asbestos was phased out of building products in the 1970s and 1980s. Fiberglass, mineral wool, and glass wool have replaced asbestos for insulation. Some products incorporate organic fibers and wood fibers. Stone fibers are used in gaskets and friction materials. Synthetic products are widely used in brake linings and bulletproof vests.

Q107: What is rabies?

Rabies is a deadly virus that attacks the central nervous system and causes encephalitis or swelling of the brain. Rabies kills 50,000 people per year, mostly (95 percent) in Asia and Africa. The vast majority (97 percent) of rabies cases result from dog bites.

Any warm-blooded animal can be infected with rabies. That includes farm animals, raccoons, skunks, and bats. Animals that rarely carry the rabies virus are squirrels, hamsters, gerbils, chipmunks, rats, mice, and rabbits.

The virus is present in the saliva of a rabid critter. When a person is bitten by an infected animal, the virus gets into muscles, where it multiplies and enters nerve endings. The virus makes its way along nerve cells toward the central nervous system of the spine and brain.

The incubation period, the time between bite and symptoms, is typically several weeks.

The first warning symptoms of rabies are malaise, fever, headaches, and flu-like symptoms. These are followed by pain, violent movements, depression, lethargy, hydrophobia, coma, and finally death. Hydrophobia (fear of water) gets people's attention. The victim has a huge increase in saliva production, and may "foam at the mouth." The dread of swallowing water is caused by painful spasms of the mouth and muscles in the throat.

Because it may take several weeks for the virus to get to the brain, there is time and opportunity to intervene by vaccination. The rabies vaccine was invented by the renowned French scientist Louis Pasteur in 1885. Pasteur took infected neural tissue from a rabbit. He allowed the rabbit tissue to weaken by drying it for a week. Then he injected a small amount of it into a nine-year-old boy who had been bitten by a rabid dog. The lad survived and lived to age 64. The vaccine is a deadened rabies virus that allows the person to build up immunity to the disease. Repeated doses are required.

The rabies vaccination is one of those rare cases where the vaccination works even after the onset of the infection. But once the virus reaches the central nervous system, it's usually curtains! Treatment is not effective, and death follows at least 99 percent of the time.

One such rare case of survival occurred in Wisconsin. In September 2004, Jeanna Giese, a 15-year-old student, picked up a bat at Saint Patrick's Church in Fond du Lac and was bitten on her left index finger. Five weeks after the incident, she was taken to Saint Agnes Hospital with a high fever, slurred speech, double vision, and jerking in her left arm. After a few days, she was diagnosed with rabies.

Her medical team decided on an experimental treatment. They put Giese in a medically induced coma to protect her brain. The hope was that she would survive long enough for her immune system to produce the antibodies needed to fight off the disease.

After six days, Giese was brought out of the coma. She was in the hospital a total of 31 days. She suffered some brain damage, had trouble with balance and running, did rehab, went back to high school, took driver's education, went to Lakeland College, and graduated in 2011. Her treatment sequence is now known as the Milwaukee protocol or Wisconsin protocol.

Q108: Why are barns red?

Settlers emigrating from Europe brought the red-barn tradition with them. Barns were a big expense for a farmer, and he wanted to protect that investment. Painting a barn made it last longer. Paint protected the barn wood from weather and mold. Farmers combined skim milk with linseed oil and lime. Linseed oil, which came from flaxseed, helped the mixture soak into the wood better. The combination of linseed oil, skim milk, and lime produced a long-lasting paint that dried quickly. It gave a plastic-like coating on the wood. The idea was to seal the wood and protect it from deteriorating from sunshine, rain, and mold or lichen that grew on wood.

Farmers added ferrous oxide, better known as rust, to the oil mixture. Rust is a poison to mold, moss, and fungi. Fungi and mold traps moisture that speeds up the decay in the wood, shortening its life. Mold is a health hazard to man and beast.

Red pigment was cheap and readily available from natural sources. Farmers found that a red barn was warmer in winter, as it absorbed more of the sun's rays than a white barn would. Wealthy farmers mixed in blood from the slaughter of farm animals, which gave the paint a deeper red color. Older barns are the true barn red. It's an earthy brownish burnt-orange red color, not the bright fire-engine red we see today. By 1900, many commercial paints added chemical pigments to get an even redder red.

But commercial paint was expensive, so some farmers turned to using whitewash, and white barns started showing up on the rural landscape. Farmers also whitewashed the interior stable, stanchions, and walls of the milking area. White interiors made for brightness and cleanliness. White barns became quite popular in Pennsylvania, Maryland, and the Shenandoah Valley of Virginia.

There is a long-held belief that barns are red so the cows can find their way home. It is just a myth. Cows are color-blind to the colors of red and green. That's why farmers don't use stoplights for their cows.

Q109: *When does a calf become a cow?*

There's a whole herd of terms to describe the bovine barnyard population. Calves are born after a gestation (pregnancy) period of about nine months. The birth of a calf is simply called calving. A calf can stand up within a few minutes of being born. It typically starts to suckle within an hour. A calf is able to follow its mother around after one week.

Calf is a term used from birth to weaning. Weaning is the separation of the suckling calf from its mother. Calves are eartagged within hours of birth, so the mother can always be identified. In some places, such as Europe, this is a legal requirement. Calves are vaccinated, and most males are castrated within two months (ouch).

A heifer is a young female calf from birth until she has a calf of her own. When the heifer becomes a mother, usually after about age two or three, we call her a cow. A castrated male is called a steer. He is destined for the meat market (a really big ouch). Cattle that end up on our table are referred to as beef cattle.

A bull is an adult male that has not been castrated. His job is to impregnate the cows, sort of a one-on-one procedure, or to provide sperm for artificial insemination.

A cow or heifer that is near calving time is referred to as a springer. A fresh cow is a cow or first-calf heifer that has recently given birth. We say the cow has freshened.

Young male calves that are born in dairy farms usually become veal. In the old West, an orphan calf that had lost its mother was termed a dogie as in "git along, little dogie."

Oxen are castrated adult male cattle. They are trained to work, and castration makes them gentler. Early American farmers used oxen as draft animals, able to haul heavy loads, plow fields, move logs, thresh grain by trampling, and pull out stumps when clearing land. Oxen were often yoked in pairs. Oxen sported horns, which allowed them to back up and not have the yoke slip off.

It was oxen that got our pioneers westward on the Oregon Trail. Horses and mules were harder to handle, spooked easily, and needed good grass for grazing. Oxen were slower, but more reliable, and much tougher than mules or horses. They could survive on rather poor grass. Oxen were easily trained, docile, and obedient.

A man or older boy led the oxen with a leash. Contrary to the depiction in movies, those hardy people did not ride in the wagons and schooners; they walked from Missouri to Oregon and California.

Any breed of cattle can be trained to be oxen, but some breeds and individuals were selected for their size, intelligence, and willingness to learn. While most oxen were castrated males, both male and female cattle were used for what we call oxen. Female oxen produced milk for those early farmers and westbound travelers. They could be bred to produce more oxen, giving the farmer replacements rather than buying new stock. At the end of their life, oxen provided food for the family.

When does a calf become a cow? A calf becomes a cow when she has her own calf.

Q110: *How is money made?*
····················

We'll assume that the question concerns the actual construction or manufacturing of currency and not earning money by working for it in a job or career. First of all, money doesn't grow on trees.

Our money is not printed on regular paper, such as typing paper or newsprint. Paper money, or paper currency, is printed on 75 percent cotton and 25 percent linen. Linen is made from flax plants. That's why we can leave a dollar bill in our pants pocket, let it through the washing machine, and have it come out good as new. If our money were printed on regular paper made from wood pulp, it would come out of the wash as a useless wet wad.

Our "paper currency" is fairly durable. The Bureau of Engraving and Printing (part of the US Department of the Treasury) claims that a bill can be folded back and forth 4,000 times without tearing. According to the bureau, it costs about ten cents to print a $1 bill, but the $100 bill comes in at a cost of 12.5 cents.

These days, schoolchildren are taught the basics of the metric system along with the old British system of weights and measures that we in the United States still use. How to teach "How much is a gram?" A dollar bill weighs 1 gram. All a teacher has to do is to haul out a any denomination bill—$1, $5, $10, $20—each of them weighs about 1 gram. So if you had 454 bills, they would weigh 454 grams, which is equal to one pound.

The US Bureau of Engraving and Printing has facilities in Washington, DC, and Fort Worth, Texas. Starting in 1929, they made all bills the same size, the size in use today. They had a lot of green ink on hand, so the story goes, so all bills were printed in that dull green tint. People liked it, and it turns out the green color holds up well against fading and chemical changes. The green color was also frustrating to early would-be counterfeiters.

Our currency was redesigned starting a little more than 15 years ago in an effort to stay ahead of counterfeiters. The first to get the new treatment was the $20 bill, the favorite target for those who want to print their own. The government engravers used color-shifting ink. Tilt the $20 bill while watching the big "20" in the lower right corner. You will notice the shift from copper to green.

Hold the bill up to a strong light and you will see a faint portrait of Andrew Jackson in the blank space right above the number 20. The printers call it a watermark, and it is visible from both sides. Those clever folks have also embedded a security thread that glows green under an ultraviolet light. Even under ordinary light, you can see it. It's about 0.75 inch (1.9 centimeters) in from the left side when looking at the Jackson side. The strip is about 1 millimeter wide and is imprinted with the words USA TWENTY alternating with a tiny flag, again visible from both sides. The bureau also uses raised printing to give the bill a distinctive feel or texture.

In subsequent years, the bureau redesigned the $50 bill in 2004, the $10 bill in 2006, the $5 bill in 2008, and the $100 bill in 2013, with a really nice rendition of Ben Franklin on the front and Independence Hall on the back. That new C-note, or Ben, is loaded with security features. A prominent wide blue stripe is placed just to the right of Ben Franklin's face. The stripe is not printed on the paper, but rather is woven into the fabric. The ribbon itself is printed with 100s and bells that interchange and move around as the $100 bill is tilted. Like the $20 bill, the $100 bill uses color-shifting ink, a watermark portrait, and a security thread. This thread glows pink under ultraviolet light. There is the printed text of THE UNITED STATES OF AMERICA on Ben Franklin's jacket collar, along with raised printing to give the paper a textured feel.

Questions have risen about the $2 bill. The $2 bill was printed from 1862 to 1966, with Thomas Jefferson on one side and Monticello on the other. The bureau stopped printing it for 10 years, and then brought out a new one in 1976 with Jefferson on one side and John Trumbull's famous painting of the drafting of the Declaration of Independence on the other side. The $2 bill is legal tender, but there are not many in circulation due to banking practices, vending machines, low printing numbers, and the problems that some people have had when they try to make purchases.

The US Bureau of Engraving and Printing employ people with all kinds of skills: chemists, police, security specialists, printers, engravers, artists, engineers, and lawyers.

Q111: *How did life start on Earth?*

. . . .

This is an excellent question with no definitive answer. Scientists do not know exactly when life started, nor the precise conditions on Earth when life began. Our ignorance is greater than our knowledge. Biology is excellent in explaining how living things work, but not good at describing how life started from non-life or inorganic material.

Humans have always asked the questions of "How did life start?" and "Are we alone in the universe?" But just as we are the first generation to leave our planet and go to the moon, we are also the first generation to try to answer those two questions scientifically.

Stanley Miller and Harold Urey in 1952 performed one early experiment. They surmised that early Earth had no oxygen but instead was composed of methane, ammonia, hydrogen, and water vapor. They sealed these gases in an airtight glass chamber and zapped the gases inside with electricity that would simulate lightning.

After one week, they found that the walls of the container had 11 of the 20 amino acids used by life on Earth. Amino acids are the building blocks of protein.

In 1961, the Catalan scientist Joan Oró added hydrogen cyanide to the original mix of gases. His experiments showed formation of the nucleic acid base adenine, which is one of the four bases that make up DNA.

Most scientists today believe that early Earth had the gases mentioned above in addition to nitrogen and carbon dioxide in the atmosphere. What about oxygen? You and I, like all animals, need oxygen. Oxygen comes from the photosynthesis of plant life. Early Earth had no oxygen, but oxygen was later produced as a result of plant growth.

We humans are largely made of carbon, hydrogen, and oxygen. In fact, plants, bacteria, worms, cows, and humans all have the same proportions of carbon, oxygen, and hydrogen. It is not too hard to make simple sugars, or bases, which are the essence of DNA. Amino acid molecules are the subunits of proteins.

We have a good sense that amino acids and nucleotide bases could have formed spontaneously in Earth conditions of the ancient past, but scientists have not yet figured out how the DNA bases and amino acids started working together to form life. How did DNA direct proteins to carry out life functions of growth and reproduction? That is a big unknown.

The definition of life must include growth and reproduction—the abilities to make more of you. Also needed is variation, the ability to introduce changes or differences in the makeup of living things. This allows natural selection can pick out those variations that are best able to survive in a changing atmosphere or new overall living conditions.

There are four main theories of how life started: metabolism, genes, ribonucleic acid (RNA), and the last universal common ancestor (LUCA).

Metabolism is the ability to break down and reassemble carbon dioxide, using some catalyst, into small organic molecules. Organic molecules became more complex, and may have evolved into life-forms. They may have assembled into primitive fatty membranes that kept certain fat-loving molecules close together and separated from water.

By a second hypothesis, and maybe helped by these membranes, genes themselves, or rather snippets of self-replicating DNA, were the first "living" organisms. The problem with this idea is that DNA cannot directly organize the manufacture of proteins.

RNA is a molecule related to DNA and found in all living organisms. Like DNA, it can be copied. As it became more complex, RNA could have directed the arrangement of amino acids into proteins that eventually built up the organisms we have today.

LUCA is the name scientists give a hypothetical common ancestor that lived more than 3 billion years ago. It may not have been the first living organism, just the first one that is ancestor to all living things. Evidence for LUCA comes from looking at the DNA of completely different organisms and mapping backward. Based on how fast we know DNA changes, how long ago could all these different living things, from plants to bacteria to animals, have started to evolve in separate directions? It's possible that a common ancestor, LUCA, may even have traveled to Earth from a distant site in the universe.

These are four educated guesses. Researchers continue to examine and test them.

What is clear is that all living things evolved from lower life-forms. Some people are uncomfortable with the word evolution. It conjures up images of apes and monkeys, and it brings up shades of the 1925 Scopes Monkey Trial in Tennessee. Some folks see evolution as a conflict between science and religion.

But evolution is simply a matter of change over eons through natural selection. We know that the genetic material of living things is always changing through mutation or through assortment when two organisms join together. Natural selection points out something that should be obvious. Genes that allow the organisms carrying them to survive and have lots of offspring will be passed on and will increase in the population. Over time, the makeup of the population will change in that direction of better survival. Ponder this idea. If we came from the mud, is that truly important? Isn't it more important that we don't slip back into the slime?

Index

A

acid 35, 36, 67, 103, 110, 137, 188, 190, 191, 192
  phosphoric acid 35, 36
airplanes 129, 208, 238
aliens 129, 130, 157, 158, 159, 165
alloys
  brass 132, 197
  bronze 183, 196
  cupronickel 197
  steel 75, 116, 158, 178, 196, 219
Alloys 196
Alzheimer's 24, 25
ammonia 31, 32, 111, 191, 206
Archimedes 84, 85, 86
  Archimedes' Principle 85
arc lamp 211, 212
arsenic 20, 31, 197
asbestos 219, 220, 221
Ashley, Robert 69
astrology 29, 164, 165
atmosphere 94, 97, 101, 102, 106, 110, 111, 112, 113, 129, 145, 192, 200, 201
atoms 101, 105, 109, 118, 127, 136, 137, 152, 160, 190, 194, 195, 196, 198, 201, 206
  electrons 101, 136
  neutrons 108
  protons 109, 194, 198, 199, 200
aurora borealis 101, 102
autism 37, 39

B

bacteria 28, 35, 37, 55, 75, 90, 103, 112, 170, 171, 172
  cholera 170
baseball 41, 49, 120, 121, 122, 123, 124

bases 89, 191
batteries 116, 136, 137, 138, 148, 188
bees 54, 55, 56, 57, 58, 119, 178
  buzzing 56
  Colony Collapse Disorder 57
  drones 55
  queen bee 55, 56
Bendectin 37, 38, 39
Big Bang 20, 80, 88, 107, 108
birds 45, 47, 50, 51, 52, 53, 54, 59, 62, 77, 119
  myoglobin 62
birth defects 37, 38, 39
black hole 20, 104, 105, 106
bones 20, 21, 22, 33, 34, 35, 36, 67, 70, 71, 90, 187, 192, 193, 194
  electrical bone stimulation 33
Borlaug, Norman 91, 92
bottles 132, 133
Boyle's Law 66
brain 21, 23, 24, 25, 26, 30, 40, 41, 76, 119, 128, 158, 160, 172, 187, 214, 221, 222
  brainstem 23, 25
  cortex 23, 32, 119
  hippocampus 25
  limbic system 23
  thalamus 41

C

Cai Lun 81
calcium 20, 21, 22, 34, 35, 36, 69, 70, 71, 187, 199
calculus 124, 125, 126
cancer 31, 32, 33, 71, 147, 194, 199, 214, 220
carbon 20, 58, 59, 66, 67, 97, 101, 103, 105, 106, 110, 111, 112, 113, 116, 137, 140, 143, 144, 145, 157, 194, 195, 196, 199, 200, 201, 202, 211, 212
carbon dating 199, 200, 202.
  See radioactivity
carbon dioxide 58, 59, 66, 67, 97, 101, 103, 106, 110, 111,

Farnsworth, Philo T. 86, 87
fat 20, 22, 45, 46, 47, 63, 68, 69,
        73, 147, 192
feces 27
Fermi, Enrico 127, 128
  Fermi question 127
fish 44, 70, 175, 179, 192
  freshwater fish 44
  saltwater fish 44
force 60, 85, 105, 109, 120, 121,
        162, 198, 209
fracking 99, 100
Franklin, Ben 117, 227
frequency 56, 118, 131, 132,
        133, 199, 216, 218, 219
frost 174, 175
fusion, thermonuclear 153

G

galaxies 20, 107, 108, 109
Galileo 204
gasoline 142, 143, 144, 145, 146,
        148, 177, 187
genes 28, 29, 171, 172
genetics 22, 68
germs 170, 172, 199
glaciers 95, 96, 97
gold 20, 21, 84, 85, 86, 184, 196,
        197
Grant, Albert 65
Gutenberg, Johannes 82

H

hair 20, 29, 30, 31, 32, 33, 68,
        70, 155, 160, 220
  hair dye 31, 32
  hair follicle 30
Hanks, Tom 84
Hanssen, Robert 139
Heisenberg Uncertainty Principle
        160
helium 105, 111, 112, 152
Hubble Space Telescope 20, 207
hydrogen 20, 32, 104, 105, 109,
        111, 112, 144, 151, 152,
        166, 190, 194, 195

I

ice 46, 70, 75, 95, 96, 97, 109,
        111, 112, 174, 175, 177,
        200, 208
impulse-momentum theorem 121
inland taipan 50
International Space Station 102,
        107

J

Jell-O 67, 68
  gelatin 67, 68
Jenner, Edward 90
jet lag 52, 53
Judson, Whitcomb 209

K

Kilauea 98
koalas 46, 47

L

lead 115, 117, 118, 137, 187,
        188, 193, 199, 201
  lead mining 188
  lead poisoning 187
Leibniz, Gottfried Wilhelm 126
lie detector 138, 139
  galvanic skin resistance 138
light 58, 94, 129, 145, 163, 183,
        192, 207
  reflection of 74, 118
lightning 68, 94, 95, 104, 211
lightsaber 161, 162
lions 48
Lovell, James, Commander 84
Lyme disease 39, 40

M

mammals 45
Mars 105, 106, 107, 109, 110,
        111
mathematics 126
McClintock, Barbara 80
melanin 29

X

Z

Larry Scheckel grew up on a family farm in the hill country of southwestern Wisconsin, one of nine children. He attended eight years of a one-room country school. After serving in the military and working as an engineer, he taught high school physics and aeronautics for thirty-eight years. He has won numerous teaching awards, authored many articles, and given presentations on science to thousands of adults and young people. Now retired from teaching, Larry enjoys bicycling, flying real and radio-controlled airplanes, and solving crossword puzzles. Larry and his wife, Ann, live in Tomah, Wisconsin, and love to travel.

Books by Larry Scheckel

Ask Your Science Teacher (2011)

Ask A Science Teacher (2013)

Seneca Seasons: A Farm Boy Remembers (2014)

I Always Wondered About That: 101 Questions and Answers About Science and Other Stuff (2017)

Murder in Wisconsin: The Clara Olson Case (2018)

I Wondered About That Too: 111 Questions and Answers About Science and Other Stuff (November, 2018)

I Just Keep Wondering: 121 Questions and Answers About Science and Other Stuff (2019)

Tumblehome's NSTA-CBC OSTB
(Outstanding Science Trade Books K-12) Award Winning Titles

Juvenile Fiction
Mosquitoes Don't Bite Me (2017) 978-1-943431-30-4. 978-1-943431-37-3
The Walking Fish (2015) 978-0-9907829-3-3, 978-0-9907829-4-0
Something Stinks! (2013) 978-0-9850008-9-9

Young Adult Non-Fiction
Magnificent Minds (2015) 978-0-9897924-7-9, 978-1-943431-25-0
Remarkable Minds (2015) 978-0-9907829-0-2, 978-1-943431-13-7

Other Tumblehome Titles

Non-Fiction Reads
I Just Keep Wondering - 121 Quesitons And Answers About Science & Other Stuff (2019)
Inventors, Makers, Barrier Breakers (2018) 978-1-943431-42-7
I Wondered About That Too - 111 Questions And Answers About Science & Other Stuff (2018) 978-1-943431-38-0
I Always Wondered About That - 101 Questions And Answers About Science & Other Stuff (2017) 978-1-943431-29-8
Dinosaur Eggs & Blue Ribbons (2015) 978-0-9897924-5-5

Fiction
Jake And The Quake (2018) 978-1-943431-39-7, 978-1-943431-40-3
Seven Stories About The Moon (science poetry, 2018) 978-1-943431-33-5
Missing Bones (2018) 978-1-943431-34-2
TimeTilter (2018) 978-1-943431-31-1
Gasparilla's Gold (2016) 978-1-943431-19-9, 978-1-943431-20-5
Bees On The Roof (2018) 978-1-943431-24-3
Talk To Me (2016) 978-1-943431-23-6

Picture Books
Waiting for Joey - An Antarctic Penguin Journal (2018) 978-1-943431-41-0
How the Dormacks Evolved Longer Backs (2018) 978-1-943431-27-4
Geology Is A Piece Of Cake (2017) 978-1-943431-28-1
How the Piloses Evolved Skinny Noses (2017) 978-1-943431-26-7
Stem Cells Are Everywhere (2016) 978-0-9897924-9-3
Seeking the Snow Leopard (2016) 978-1-943431-16-8
Painting In The Dark - Esref Armagan, Blind Artist (2016)
978-1-943431-15-1, 978-1-943431-14-4
Elizabeth's Constellation Quilt (2015) 978-0-9907829-1-9

GALACTIC ACADEMY OF SCIENCE, "G.A.S.", SERIES

CLINTON AND MAE'S MISSIONS:

The Desperate Case of the Diamond Chip
978-0-9850008-0-6
The Vicious Case of the Viral Vaccine
978-0-9850008-7-5
The Baffling Case of the Battered Brain
978-0-9897924-1-7
The Perilous Case of the Zombie Potion
978-0-9897924-3-1
The Contaminated Case of the Cooking Contest
978-0-9907829-2-6
The Secret Case of the Space Station Stowaways
978-1-943431-18-2

ANITA AND BENSON'S MISSIONS:

The Furious Case of the Fraudulent Fossil
978-0-9850008-5-1
The Harrowing Case of the Hackensack Hacker
978-0-9850008-8-2
The Confounding Case of the Climate Crisis
978-0-9897924-4-8

ELLA AND SHOMARI'S MISSION:

The Cryptic Case of the Coded Fair
978-0-9897924-2-4